REBRAND YOU

REBRAND YOU

A PROVEN GUIDE TO REDESIGN YOUR LIFE
ON PURPOSE

CLARITY | ACTION | EVOLUTION

ALEXIS CASTORINA

REBRAND YOU: A Proven Guide to Redesign Your Life – On Purpose
Published by Cymatic Media
Cave Creek, AZ
CymaticMedia.com
Copyright ©2026 by Alexis Castorina. All rights reserved.

No part of this book may be reproduced in any form or by any mechanical means, including information storage and retrieval systems without permission in writing from the publisher/author, except by a reviewer who may quote passages in a review.

All images, logos, quotes, and trademarks included in this book are subject to use according to trademark and copyright laws of the United States of America.

ISBN 979-8-9992301-0-2 (paperback)
ISBN 979-8-9992301-1-9 (eBook)
ISBN 979-8-9992301-2-6 (hardcover)

SELF-HELP / General
SELF-HELP / Personal Growth / General

Cover and interior design by Laura Duffy, copyright owned by Alexis Castorina.

Photography by Quianna Marie of Quianna Marie Photography and FemForce Shoots Photography.

Disclaimer:
This book is intended to educate, inspire, and support personal growth. It does not offer medical, psychological, or professional advice. The author and publisher are not responsible for any actions taken based on the content of this book. Always consult a qualified professional for any physical, emotional, or medical concerns. Use of the information is at the reader's discretion and risk. No guarantees of outcomes are made or implied.

QUANTITY PURCHASES: Schools, companies, professional groups, clubs, and other organizations may qualify for special terms when ordering quantities of this title.

For information, visit: alexiscastorina.com
Follow on Instagram at @alexiscastorina
All rights reserved by Alexis Castorina and Cymatic Media.

Dedication

To the gritty souls who rise with resilience; find clarity in the midst of uncertainty; and remain anchored in truth, justice, and love. May your unwavering belief in yourself lead you to a life of purpose and possibility.

CONTENTS

Foreword
by Alessia Citro ix

Introduction:
Your Rebrand Journey Starts Here xi

Step 1: Reflect and Research Your Current State 1
- Chapter 1: Reflect on What's Happening FOR You 3
- Chapter 2: Self-Assessment Tools and Exercises 23
- Chapter 3: Gathering Feedback from Others 39

Step 2: Examine and Analyze Your Findings 51
- Chapter 4: Spotting Patterns and Themes 53
- Chapter 5: Conducting Your Personal SWOT 75

Step 3: Brainstorm Potential New Beginnings 85
- Chapter 6: Envisioning Your Ideal Life 87
- Chapter 7: Exploring New Possibilities 95

Step 4: Reframe, Reprogram, Rewire 129
- Chapter 8: Why Mindset Is Essential to Success 131
- Chapter 9: Reframe—Change the Lens 137
- Chapter 10: Reprogram—Rewrite the Script 143
- Chapter 11: Rewire—Make it Stick 157

Step 5: Activate Your Aligned Strategy **171**
- Chapter 12: Focus on Your "Why" and Values 173
- Chapter 13: Goal Setting and Action Planning 183
- Chapter 14: Lifestyle Design 205
- Chapter 15: Transforming Your Identity
  and Personal Brand 211

Step 6: Network and Build Your Community **227**
- Chapter 16: The Power of Relationships 229
- Chapter 17: Finding Your People and Building
  Your Community 239

Step 7: Develop a Growth Mindset **253**
- Chapter 18: Test and Learn 255
- Chapter 19: Embrace Lifelong Learning,
  Change, and Growth 269

Your Rebrand Launch and Evolution **283**

Resources **289**

Work with Me **291**

Acknowledgments **295**

Foreword

When Alexis asked me to write this foreword, I didn't hesitate. How often does a former marketing executive of a major fintech brand hand you her brainchild and say, "Will you tee this up?" Then I read the early draft, and it blew me away. This book is electric—clear, punchy, and practical in a way most books only hope to be. Best of all, it offers a blueprint to a reality all of us will face sooner or later: the need to reinvent ourselves.

I know reinvention firsthand. I've lived both sides: climbing the ladder in high-tech sales and later stepping out to create something of my own. Which is why *Rebrand YOU* resonated so deeply with me. This book doesn't prescribe one path over another. It's not about choosing corporate or entrepreneurship. It's about choosing yourself—then bringing yourself along, wherever you go.

I wish I'd had this framework back when burnout and self-doubt were eating me alive in an executive role. Yes, the job was demanding. But the bigger issue was how little of me I was bringing to it. I could power through back-to-back meetings and quarterly pressure, but I was starving for impact, wholeness, and the energy to actually enjoy the life I was building. At the time, I thought my desires were at odds with each other. They weren't. What was missing was alignment—refining my identity so I could choose environments that fit me, instead of contorting myself to fit them and paying the price.

That's why Alexis's approach is so powerful. She doesn't separate career from health, mindset from spirit. She knows the only change that actually sticks is the kind that accounts for all of you. With her framework, she blends strategy with soul, giving you the tools to reposition yourself with depth, direction, and power. Since then, I've rebranded myself more than once. First, as an author, podcaster, speaker, and coach. And now, back in corporate tech—this time with clarity, gratitude, and boundaries I didn't have before. And most importantly, the ability to bring all of me without apology. Reinvention isn't one-and-done. It's a lifelong rhythm of returning to who you are, then showing up accordingly.

And it's not just personal—it's cultural. In today's world, where the average person has nine different jobs before age thirty-five, reinvention isn't optional. The pace of change is only accelerating. The old model—stick to one title, one path, one identity—no longer exists. The people who will thrive now and beyond are the ones who know how to evolve on purpose and recalibrate without losing their center.

That's what makes Alexis the perfect guide for this work. She's lived it—career pivots, identity shifts, seasons of personal death and rebirth. Which is why this book carries not just strategies, but the kind of hard-earned wisdom you can only get from someone who's been there.

So if you've ever thought *I can't keep doing this, but I don't know where to start,* you're in the right place. Let Alexis guide you. Read this book, apply it, and let it change the way you see yourself. Because your next chapter doesn't start with a new job title or a shinier LinkedIn headline. It starts when you remember who you are—and decide to live from there.

—Alessia Citro, author of bestseller *Higher Self Habits: The Scientific, Strategic, and Spiritual Framework to Get Out of Your Own Way—For Good* and host of the podcast *INHABIT*

Introduction: Your Rebrand Journey Starts Here

"It's time for a rebrand!" Even if you're not a marketer, you've likely heard that phrase. And, guess what? I bet you've rebranded yourself a few times and didn't even realize that's what you were doing.

Businesses must evolve their identities to adapt to planned or unplanned changes, which requires them to rethink their market positioning and brand strategy. And so do people. That's right. You're a brand, hun.

Whether you're a global brand or just trying to figure out your next chapter, rebranding is about evolution. It's about recognizing when an old identity—whether it's a name, a role, or even a mindset—no longer fits.

It's not easy.

People might resist your change. Hell, *YOU* might resist your change. But staying stuck in a version of yourself that doesn't feel right? That's harder.

Who Is the Weirdo Writing This Book?

That would be me. Hi, I'm Alexis.

I've been rebranding myself for as long as I can remember—even though I didn't realize that's what I was doing—until I decided that is EXACTLY what I'm doing. Stay with me…

- I rebranded myself from being the "poor kid" to the "popular kid."

- I rebranded myself from "the cheerleader" to "the rebellious partier."

- I rebranded myself from "hanging with the wrong crowd" to "hanging with honor society nerds."

- I rebranded myself from "journalist" to "marketer."

- I rebranded myself from "engaged" to "single."

- I rebranded myself from "corporate ladder climber" to "emerging multidimensional entrepreneur," which is where this rebrand story will begin.

When Life Forces Us to Rebrand, It's a HUGE Opportunity (Even Though It Scares Us)

Let's be honest. So many of us are living on autopilot. We let our past choices, emotional baggage, and unconscious programming define our personal brand, career, and how we live our lives. We never check in with ourselves, but we keep powering through.

Exhausted. Overstimulated. Overachieving. Overthinking. Perfectionist. If any of these words resonate with you, I see you.

We have a nagging sense that we're not living up to our full potential, but we feel so exhausted by the simple act of surviving—aka going to work, taking care of our family and pets, trying to maintain friendships, exercising, and on and on and on—that we simply don't even have the bandwidth to explore alternative realities and options for ourselves.

According to a recent Gallup poll,[1] only 31 percent of US employees were engaged in their work, with 17 percent actively disengaged. This means nearly half of the workforce (48 percent) is not engaged or is actively disengaged, highlighting why so many feel stuck, burned out, and uncertain about how to move forward.

Until the universe aggressively forces you to move forward (after trying to get your attention in more subtle, gentler ways for a while, but you kept ignoring them and your intuition), alas, the hard way it is.

That's what happened to me.

In 2022, I thought I had finally "made it." I was at the top of my corporate career, working for the fastest-growing financial technology company in the United States. I had a corner office—with a window. I was winning awards, leading high-profile brand marketing projects, brokering partnerships with professional sports teams and influencers, and living the life I thought I wanted.

But then, life threw me a curveball. After ignoring the subtle whispers of the universe and my own intuition that something wasn't quite right for a few years, a series of traumatic events shattered my identity.

It was sudden. It was shocking. And it forced me to face my fears, uncover my baggage, rewire my mind, and figure out who I was going to be in the next chapter.

It's time for a rebrand, I thought to myself. That thought led to my aha moment.

What if I took the fundamentals of success in marketing and applied them to my life?

And that's when I decided:

I'm going to treat MYSELF like the most important brand campaign of my career.

---

[1] Jim Harter, "U.S. Employee Engagement Sinks to 10-Year Low," *Gallup*, January 13, 2025, https://www.gallup.com/workplace/654911/employee-engagement-sinks-year-low.aspx.

Drawing on the principles of marketing, positive psychology, neuroscience, and a touch of metaphysical spirituality, I developed a framework that helped me rebrand my mind, body, and spirit. It transformed me into the happiest, healthiest version of myself I've ever been. And now, I'm sharing that framework with you.

The REBRAND Framework

This book is your step-by-step guide to rebranding your life. Just like a company rebrands to stay relevant and aligned with its goals, you can rebrand yourself to create a life and career that truly reflect who you are and what you want.

The **REBRAND** Framework will take you through seven powerful steps to help you reflect, refine, and redesign your path:

Reflect and research your current state
Examine and analyze your findings
Brainstorm potential new beginnings
Reframe, reprogram, rewire
Activate your aligned strategy
Network and build your community
Develop a growth mindset

Each section will guide you through specific steps, blending marketing and branding concepts, personal stories, mindset shifts, neuroscience, metaphysical principles, and actionable strategies to help you gain clarity on various dimensions of yourself so you can redesign and relaunch a personal brand and lifestyle that feels fulfilling and authentic to your life's purpose and desires.

The REBRAND Framework is a marketing-inspired approach to personal and professional reinvention.

I'm talking about a marketing plan for your life, my friend. Think marketing strategy meets personal development. Yeah, iconic stuff like that. Because I truly believe you are iconic. Every single one of us already is. We simply need to tap into that higher level of awesomeness to access our authentic icon status. And, without a playbook on how to do it, the struggle can be real.

That's why I'm sharing the REBRAND Framework.

When we get playful with life and treat it like the first time we played Mario Kart on Super Nintendo (wassup, Millennials and Gen Xers), damn, it starts to get really good. And fun! When you treat it as such and finally make it to Nana's age, you'll look back on your life when you're sitting in your rocking chair (or in your spaceship on Mars, at the rate things are advancing), and you'll be like "I remember when that silly broad Alexis taught me how to outsmart the mental villain that was blocking me from reaching the final level of greatness: my authentic expression and achieving my highest potential." Pure joy.

In this book, you'll learn how to:

- Reflect on your current state and uncover what's holding you back.

- Examine your findings and identify patterns that no longer serve you.

- Brainstorm new possibilities and create a vision for your future.

- Reframe and reprogram your mind to see challenges as opportunities.

- Activate your strategy and optimize for improvement.

- Network and build a community that supports your growth.

- Develop a growth mindset and embrace lifelong learning and evolution.

You'll also hear personal anecdotes, comedic insights (yes, I became a paid comedian after going through this framework), career research, neuroscience studies, Neuro-Linguistic Programming (NLP) principles, and marketing secrets that will help you rebrand yourself from the inside out.

While all the steps to your rebrand and transformation are clearly outlined in this book, I also created the *Rebrand YOU Companion Workbook* that you can purchase as a complement to this book to make things even easier for you to complete the exercises. The companion workbook is not meant to replace this book. It is meant to be an additional resource to keep you individually organized. It's also an awesome tool and guide to use with a friend, group, or book club. Why rebrand alone when you can do it with a community and accountability buddies!

You can access the companion workbook in the Resources section of this book or at RebrandYouBook.com.

What This Book Will Do for You

This isn't another book about personal branding or the same personal development books you've read a million times that pump you up but then leave you hanging on the HOW to execute. This book is the enterprise-level objectives and key results (OKR) and SMART goal/three-to-five year-to-eternity plan—combined—along with the strategy and tactics to rebrand you from the inside out. I'm talking specific steps along with ChatGPT prompts, with instructions like "create this folder on your Google Drive and label it this." Tactical and practical, my friend.

Told you. This book is "different, it's different. It's different." (If you sang that part out loud, we should totally be friends.)

By the end of this book, you'll have the tools to help you:

- Identify areas of your personal and professional life that need to be redesigned and relaunched.

- Reconnect with your authentic self and what lights you up.

- Gain clarity on your passions, talents, and life vision.

- Understand why mindset is foundational to our happiness and ability to manifest our desired reality.

- Break through limiting beliefs that keep you stuck.

- Build the foundation for a personal brand, community, career, or business that aligns with your values and highest potential.

- Navigate change and low points in your life confidently by taking a positive approach to controlling your thoughts, behaviors, and actions.

- Design your ideal lifestyle aligned with your values and desires.

- Find your people, the like-minded souls on a path to authentic awesomeness like you.

- Embrace lifelong learning, growth, and future rebrands and launches.

My intention for writing this book is for you to finish the last page, shut the book, and feel empowered to grow personally and professionally in a way that's fulfilling, exciting, and truly you.

I needed this book so badly, and I know so many others do too.

Don't Stay Stuck—Reimagine, Reinvent, and Rebrand!

You don't have to settle for a life that feels out of alignment. You don't have to do anything just because that's how you've always done it. You don't have to stay stuck in a story that doesn't feel like yours. You have the power to create a new story—one that's authentic, fulfilling, and uniquely yours.

It's time to redesign and hard launch into living your best life!

You're not too old. You're not too young. You're not too late. You're not too poor. You're not too "anything."

You got this!

So, let's leave the excuses at the door, follow the steps I've outlined in this book, and freaking do it!

You ready? Let's rebrand you!

STEP 1

REFLECT AND RESEARCH YOUR CURRENT STATE

E

B

R

A

N

D

CHAPTER 1

Reflect on What's Happening FOR You

How often do you check in with yourself? And I don't mean checking there's no food stuck in your teeth or a sniff test to verify that you DID in fact put deodorant on this morning. But like *REALLY* check in with yourself?

If you're like me and most other people spinning on this magical ball in the universe, it's probably close to never. Between work, our daily household duties—like cooking, keeping the house tidy, exercising, family obligations, trying to have a social life, and our "self-care"—when do we even have the luxury of checking in with ourselves when we're always "ON" with no break?

Annoying, right?

Well, it seems like if you're reading this book right now, you may have a few free moments to yourself. So, now that I have your attention, I'm going to ask you this question, and I want you to take a few moments to think about your honest response.

I don't want to get all Jenna Kutcher-y with this, so I'll rephrase her question from her popular book *How Are You, Really?* to my own version:

How the hell are ya? No bullshit. Circle of trust. Swear to God. For real.

How do you feel about the way you're living, loving, and showing up in the world? How do you feel about the way you're showing up for yourself?

Are you happy? Are you anxious? Are you tired? Are you overwhelmed? Cranky? Excited? Bored? Energized? Pissed off? Demotivated? Unappreciated?

What is your vibe?

Here's a big one: Do you even know yourself enough to answer that question?

… Whew. If that was a lot, I get it. And if you needed a tissue after those moments of self-reflection, I see you. And I'm sending you so much love.

Think of your brand as the operating system running your life. It's not just the wallpaper or the apps (your TikTok, your Instagram profile, your LinkedIn bio). It's the whole system: how you show up, what you value, how you make decisions, and how others experience you. In the twenty-four hours we're allotted every day, most of us are living on autopilot. Rarely do we proactively take the time to check in with ourselves to see if things are still aligned with our vision (if we even have one). We don't pause to see how we're tracking or if we want to recast a new vision or make some adjustments.

We don't pause long enough to see if our current brand—our operating system—is still strong or if it's time for a rebrand.

In the corporate world, we'd do a hindsight or postmortem meeting a few days after a big event was over to see what went well, what didn't go well, and what opportunities for improvements could be made for the following year's event. We proactively reflected.

Unfortunately, for so many of us, the only time we pause and slow down is when we're forced to. It's reactive. Usually, that forced pause comes from an unexpected, negative event that knocks us down.

Sound familiar?

Well, that's exactly what happened to me. I was blindsided like a smack to the face that hurt like hell but was the best damn thing to happen to me—a realization I discovered after my personal postmortem meeting.

My "State" in 2022

For the first half of 2022, I was on top of the world. The COVID craziness was finally dissipating, and people were traveling and attending large events again. I was jet-setting across the country for work, staying in fancy boutique hotels in cities like New York, LA, and San Francisco, winning awards, being interviewed by media, speaking on panels and podcasts, and brokering high-profile brand partnerships that made a positive impact on my company's bottom line and served the greater good.

My career was everything I had worked so hard for. I was in a marketing leadership role at a fintech brand that was quickly on its way to becoming a household name.

Not only was I part of the original team to bring this brand to market—the team that got to vote on what we named the brand and product suite—but I was also in a marketing leadership role that I essentially crafted and developed for myself (after years of trying to make the case to the leadership team of why it was needed).

Then, in the span of a few months, everything changed.

A series of three traumatic events shattered the trajectory I was on. It was as if the universe had other plans for me. My identity, sense of safety, and everything I had worked so hard for my entire life were suddenly in question.

First, a Car Accident

My friend was getting married in Mexico in a few days, so of course, I needed to get a mani and pedi in preparation. After leaving the nail salon, I made an impromptu decision to visit my mom, who lived only a few miles away.

I got off the exit for my mom's house. As I turned left at the intersection, the driver in the lane next to me, who was also supposed to be turning left, unexpectedly continued straight through. His Jeep hit the driver's side of my truck at about 40 mph, and the force of the collision sent his vehicle careening into a concrete barrier at the corner. My airbags deployed, and miraculously I was unharmed.

The other vehicle had to be cut open to get the driver out. He was unconscious and put onto a stretcher and rushed to the hospital across the street. I was put into the back of a police car.

I was assured I wasn't under arrest; it was just a precaution given the severity of the accident while we waited for detectives to arrive on the scene. Two hours and two sobriety tests later, I was permitted to leave, but my truck was not. It was inoperable and needed to be taken to an impound lot for evidence.

Be OK. Be OK. PLEASE! Be OK was the mantra on repeat inside my head. My heart raced. My breathing was so shallow it felt like I couldn't get enough air inside my lungs. The police and first responders gave me no information about the other driver's condition, who he was, or even where my truck was being taken. For a person who relishes having control and detailed information, I had none. The discomfort of the unknown was suffocating. Panic. Anxiety. Fear.

The next day, after my own detective work, I found out the other driver had died. All I kept thinking was, *Why did he die, and why did I survive without even a scratch?* I also wondered, *What would've happened to me if I had just one glass of champagne at the nail salon?*

And while the accident wasn't my fault, a few months later, I found out I was being sued in a wrongful death lawsuit.

Second, a Career Transition

In the summer of 2022, I decided to make some extra income and do freelance marketing again to expedite the path to realizing my dream of owning a cabin in Flagstaff, Arizona.

Rather than being a 1099 contractor, I created an LLC. No sooner did I officially form my business entity, the universe started sending me referrals for marketing support. One of those clients wanted to bring me on as a consultant and, as a newer business, couldn't afford my rate but offered me an equity package. While I was negotiating the agreement, I was worried I might have to turn down the opportunity due to a potential conflict of interest with my employer.

But the universe removed that barrier for me.

The following week, after returning from Ohio—where I'd been honored on a massive stage for leading a consumer education campaign that won Best Consumer Brand Campaign of the Year—and then flying out the next day to an experiential event in Kentucky I'd championed (which, by the way, turned out to be a huge success), I was fired from my corporate job. A total shock. Out of nowhere. Over the phone. No meaningful explanation. No severance.

Oddly, just days before I was fired, I was given a substantial raise and more budget to hire another person. How does this happen to a well-liked, loyal high performer who gave so much of herself for seven years to the company? Someone the CEO publicly praised on LinkedIn just weeks before being terminated?

The answer, I've come to believe, is God, Source, the Universe, Creator, insert whatever word personally resonates with you. Sometimes, life forces you out of a situation that no longer serves you, even when it makes no logical sense. The shock was real. One moment I was at the height of my career; the next, I felt exiled from the community and reputation I'd spent years nurturing. Yet, even in the midst of that overwhelming loss, I'm grateful God/the universe provided a soft landing.

The very next week, I seamlessly transitioned into a fractional chief marketing officer (CMO) role for a financial services consulting firm and, shortly after that, took on marketing consulting work for a global consumer packaged goods company where my former colleague was the CMO. On paper, it looked like a natural step up the career ladder, from senior director to CMO, without missing a beat or ever being unemployed. This is the power of your network, which I'll teach you about in Step 6 of the REBRAND Framework.

Third, a Health Scare

My health started to take a turn for the worse. I thought perhaps it was just burnout, or depression and anxiety from the car accident. Or the shame of being fired. I thought it was fear that I would lose this multimillion-dollar lawsuit and all of my assets that I worked so hard for. My beautiful house. The condo I bought for my mom to live in. My retirement savings. My truck. My dignity. My everything.

You see, one of the biggest fears I have in life is being poor because of the poverty I experienced in my childhood. Financial security and stability are something I've been striving for my entire life. And like my job, I feared my wealth was yet another thing that could suddenly be taken from me, that I'd have no control over.

However, the physical and mental symptoms were caused by something bigger than anxiety. My symptoms were caused from breast implant illness.

Since getting breast implants in 2011, my body was on a slow drip of poison. Every day, my body was struggling to operate normally as it attempted to fight the foreign substances in my body with an inflammatory response to protect my vital organs and systems. By the way, all I wanted was a breast lift, but some doctors talk you into things and assure you of the safety of the medical device or protocol after you express your concerns, gaslighting you into ignoring your intuition or peer-reviewed studies you found buried on page twenty of the Google search engine results.

I knew something wasn't right six months after getting the implants. I'll never forget the day I was in line to enter Heinz Field (as a Pittsburgher, I will always call it that; sorry not sorry, Acrisure Stadium) to attend a Steelers game. When the security guard asked me to raise my arms above my head so he could scan me with his wand to ensure I wasn't trying to smuggle in a weapon, I couldn't raise my arms.

What in the actual fuck? I thought.

After the game, I made an appointment with my primary care physician. She said my muscles were probably just sore from lifting heavy weights that week, but she'd run some blood tests to rule anything out.

As I was awaiting the blood test results, the pain in my joints became more extreme, and my muscles felt weak. My doctor had me come in to read me the test results.

"You have tested positive for ANA antibodies and your sed rate is high," she said. *Huh?* She could've been speaking Mandarin as far as I was concerned.

"I'd like you to see a rheumatologist for further testing," she said. "And I don't want you panicking and googling things before your appointment, OK?"

"OK," I agreed, with my fingers proverbially crossed behind my back.

It was the fucking breast implants. I was perfectly fine before them. And then after I got them, my body went from an athletic look to swollen and bloated. Not only did I wake up with boobs larger than agreed upon that did not look proportionate to my small five foot two frame, but I also became swollen and bloated-looking on top of that. And no diet tricks helped.

Anyway, I found a few peer-reviewed studies buried deep in Google search results. I printed them out and brought them with me to my first rheumatologist appointment. The thesis of the studies was that silicone breast implants had a positive correlation with the diagnosis of autoimmune diseases in women.[2]

My rheumatologist, a man who looked to be in his mid-sixties, assured me the FDA took them off the market for several years, worked out the kinks, and they were deemed "safe" again, so that couldn't be it. My intuition said otherwise, but the lab coat effect is real, so I conceded and nodded in agreement.

After additional tests, he couldn't quite figure out what I had, so he slapped the diagnosis mixed connective tissue disease (MCTD) on my chart. MCTD is an autoimmune disease that isn't quite in a class of its own because it's a hodgepodge of symptoms from autoimmune diseases like lupus, scleroderma, arthritis, Raynaud's syndrome, and other inflammatory conditions that cause joint pain and disruption to your kidneys and other organs.

He said he'd prescribe me a pill called hydroxychloroquine to fight the inflammation, but it could also cause me to go blind after years of continual use, so I'd need to get a special eye exam every year to keep an eye on things (pun intended).

Over the next ten years, I battled with joint pain, fatigue, inflammation, acne, rashes, depression, anxiety, urinary and kidney infections, weight gain, and brain fog. It was like playing Whack-A-Mole trying to uncover the root cause.

Thousands of dollars and tears shed later, a conversation with a friend and former colleague visiting Scottsdale, Arizona, for a conference would change my health and life after I complained to her about a rash on my face after a day at the Fairmont Scottsdale Princess resort pool.

---

2 Abdulla Watad et al., "Silicone breast implants and the risk of autoimmune/rheumatic disorders: a real-world analysis," *International Journal of Epidemiology* 47, no. 6 (2018): 1846–1854, https://academic.oup.com/ije/article/47/6/1846/5133598.

My friend looked down at my chest and then looked up at my face, and she asked, "Do you watch *The Bachelor* or *The Bachelorette?*"

"No," I replied, secretly judging my brainiac friend for watching reality trash TV—yet conveniently forgetting about my personal obsession with *The Jersey Shore* and *The Jersey Shore: Family Vacation.*

"Do you know who Clare Crawley is," she asked.

I shook my head no, wondering where she was going with this.

"Have you ever heard of breast implant illness?"

My entire body flooded with chills. I had goosebumps so hard that my skin probably looked like freshly plucked chicken. Tingles flooded up and down my entire body. And in that moment, the phone in her suite rang, snapping me back from my disassociated state. "Your driver is here, ma'am."

I didn't even have a chance to thank her for bestowing upon me a diagnosis and root cause I'd been searching over a decade for. We quickly hugged, I gathered my things, and I was transported to the other side of the resort where my truck was parked.

That was exactly what had been causing me so much misery for the last ten years. I freaking knew it! I intuitively knew from the moment I couldn't raise my arms at the Steelers game the breast implants were the problem.

When I got home that night, I immediately begin my crusade of research, found a breast implant illness support group on Facebook, and scheduled three consultations for explant surgery. These toxic bags were going to come out.

They say things happen in threes, so I was confident this was the final event in the trifecta of curveballs being thrown at me.

My familiar method of dealing with negative things in my life up until this point was to rely on my resiliency and thick skin: Be strong (hide your painful emotions), focus on something else (deflect to what I could control whether that was food or exercise) and power through (operate from adrenaline-fueled fear).

That old strategy always left me feeling depleted and exhausted because I never reached the proverbial finish line. I'd need a new strategy this time. I couldn't speed up and power through. I'd have to do the opposite: slow down.

Coincidence or Divine Intervention? A New Strategy Emerged

I intuitively knew all of these events weren't a coincidence. My gut was telling me they were a forced way to get me to slow down because I had been moving too fast for far too long. My instincts told me to use this opportunity to examine my life. I knew if I challenged my limiting beliefs and reframed my mindset, I would uncover the blessing in disguise.

... If only I had a blueprint or playbook on how to find out what it was as quickly as possible. "Hey, God. I'd like to order a step-by-step plan for figuring my shit out." Alas, the divine realm doesn't work like Amazon Prime.

Instead of feeling sorry for myself and asking,
"Why is this happening to me?" I asked,
"What is this teaching me?"

As a lifelong personal development and psychology junkie, I learned a thing or two about the importance of regulating our nervous system—especially during really difficult times in our lives.

So, my initial strategy to figure out what this was teaching me was to first *prime* myself to be in an elevated, high-vibe, high-frequency state of being.

To receive messages and downloads from my higher self, the Holy Spirit, God, the Universe, Source, Creator, whatever you like to call it (I personally use all of these terms!), I knew I had to slow down, and this felt so uncomfortable to the overachieving people pleaser in me. I embraced surrender and forgiveness. I forgave myself for my past choices and forgave the people I perceived to have "wronged me."

I gave myself grace, and instead of fighting back with lawsuits, I surrendered everything to the Universe/God to sort out. I intuitively knew I needed to take a different approach. I would go against the grain and the playbook I was advised to follow by so many people in my ear, and I wouldn't retaliate. I would have an open heart and send love to those who were trying to tear me down.

Control What You Can, and Surrender the Rest

I mainly surrendered everything, but I knew it was up to me to take control of the things I could, like my physical and mental health. I scheduled a surgery to remove my breast implants, hoping that after the explant, my symptoms would subside and I'd feel better. I reduced my board commitments and client work to focus on healing my mind, body, and spirit.

Here's what else I did:

For My MIND (Mental)
I detoxed my mind by avoiding negative news and content that made me feel bad or lowered my frequency. (You'll learn more about the science behind this in Chapter 11.) I read and listened to a ton of uplifting books and podcasts, which deepened my obsession with neuroscience.

I love comedy and know laughing raises your frequency, so I embraced a longtime bucket list item and took improv and stand-up comedy classes. (FYI, I'm now a paid comedian and speaker, and I have a keynote on conscious comedy about using humor as a tool for healing, transformation, and business growth.)

For My BODY (Physical)
After I was cleared to start working out again after surgery, I had a deeper appreciation for my health and body. I began saying daily affirmations like "Thank you, God, I love my body." I appreciated the imperfections, scars, and found beauty in it all. I wasn't focused on my aesthetics, but rather my vitality.

I wasn't focused on losing weight. I was focused on honoring my body and getting stronger. So, I joined a fitness challenge at my gym and lost sixteen pounds while building muscle. I won first place and a cold plunge and sauna for my house!

For My SPIRIT (Spiritual)
I started consuming a broader range of spiritual content, both new age and traditional religious texts. I read *The Bible* and *A Course in Miracles* cover to cover. I watched videos of people who had near-death experiences. I read about the wisdom and regrets of people who were in hospice, ready to die. Things they wish they had done or realized sooner. And I vowed to heed their advice so I could lie on my deathbed with "No Ragrets," as Scottie P. would say. No, not even one.

The Opportunity

And just like that, the life I had built up until that point was gone. Oddly, I was handling it much better than I normally would've. I had been reading enough positive and spiritual content after I got fired and was being sued that I was already leaning into faith. I knew this healing time and slow era was a gift.

I even recalled a psychic reading a few years prior, and the notion of a sabbatical came up a lot. Was this it? Was this the sabbatical that would allow me to slow down, reflect, and figure out what I really wanted from my life? God knows I never would've slowed down otherwise at the pace I was going being driven by fear and ego and a constant feeling I needed to prove my worth and add value to everything I touched, have all the answers, and execute everything perfectly with poise, polished nails, a sleek wardrobe, typo-free with perfect margins and alignment, anticipating every possible question, and having a contingency plan for scenarios A–Z. Not this time. There would be no playbook. No contingency plan.

That's when it hit me: What if I treated my life like the most important brand campaign of my career?

What if I combined my twenty years of marketing expertise with all the knowledge I gained over the years as a self-help, positive psychology junkie? I could create a framework just like I would a campaign brief for my company or client.

In marketing, every campaign starts with a clear challenge or problem statement (a concise description of a current, specific issue or challenge the campaign aims to address, aka the problem to solve) and an objective (the desired outcome or result the campaign aims to achieve).

I realized I could apply the same strategic thinking to my own life.

- I am the business.

- **My goals** are the business's objectives.

- **My problems/obstacles/pain points** are the business's challenges.

- **My purpose** is the business's mission.

So, I became my own project. I designed a unique framework as a guide and blueprint to help me reach my objective: to design a life I love that is aligned with a new high-vibe version of myself.

I created a marketing plan for my life—where marketing strategy meets personal development. A new campaign. A rebrand.

Reflection Uncovers Your Rebrand Challenge and Objective

Reflection is often the most overlooked step in the process of transformation, but it's also the most important. Without it, you're just throwing spaghetti at the wall and hoping something sticks.

As I learned during my own journey, slowing down and reflecting on your life is the key to uncovering your truth. It's the foundation for everything that comes next.

In a world that glorifies hustle and busyness, it can feel uncomfortable to slow down and sit with your thoughts. As author Brené Brown[3] says, "We stay so busy that the truth of our lives can't catch up."

Many of us avoid reflection because we're afraid of what we might find. We're afraid to admit that we're unhappy, unfulfilled, or off track. But you can't create a roadmap for where you want to go if you don't know where you are. You need to get real with yourself. Ask the tough questions. Uncover the truth about where you are. Then set an intention for where you want to go.

---

[3] Brené Brown, quoted in "Brené Brown on the Power of Vulnerability," *The Washington Post*, October 2012.

Reflection gives you clarity. It helps you identify what's working, what's not, and what needs to change. It's the first step in rebranding your life and creating a future that feels authentic and fulfilling.

For example, one of my clients, "Jen," came to me feeling stuck in a job she'd outgrown. Through honest reflection, she realized her real challenge wasn't just the job, it was her fear of starting over in a new industry. Once she named that, her objective became clear: to find a role that excited her and allowed her to grow, even if it meant stepping outside her industry and comfort zone.

Another client, "James," discovered through reflection that his biggest challenge was burnout from saying yes to everything. His objective shifted from "get promoted" to "create boundaries and reclaim his time."

Every great marketing campaign starts with a clear understanding of the challenge and the objective. The same is true for your life.

Here's how to use this framework for yourself:

Reflect: Assess how life is going, think about what you want, how things are, and where you're currently headed.

Identify the Challenge: What's standing in your way? What's the biggest friction point or obstacle you're facing right now?

Set the Objective: What does success look like for you? What's the clear, measurable outcome you want to achieve?

Some people prefer to start with the objective and then identify the challenges, and that's valid too. But for this framework, I've found that starting with the challenge helps clarify what needs to change before you set your sights on the goal.

As you reflect, you'll likely start to surface challenges (problems) and the objectives (desired outcomes) you want to experience as a result of overcoming the challenges.

If you're reading this book, you already know you're ready for a big shift. You're ready to take action. You're ready to intentionally redesign your life. Reflection will help you identify the impetus behind your desire to rebrand, if it's not already glaringly obvious to you.

Maybe you're feeling stuck in your career, or you're struggling to balance work and family. Maybe you're burned out, overwhelmed, or unsure of what you want next. Maybe you're afraid artificial intelligence is going to make your current job and career path obsolete. Maybe you're worried that companies will realize they can achieve their goals faster and cheaper by outsourcing your job and entire department to specialized overseas labor. Maybe you just got laid off or fired like I did.

As your mind wanders, begin to think about what you desire (your objective). What do you want to achieve? What does success look like for you? Maybe you want to find a career that aligns with your passions. Maybe you want to feel more present with your family. Or maybe you just want to feel like yourself again.

To help give you some inspo, here is how I reflected and crafted my challenge and objective:

Reflection: I felt like I had scarlet letters branded on me spelling out the word *FIRED*. Even if I wanted to get another corporate job, which I wasn't sure I did, would they even hire me if they checked and saw that I had been involuntarily terminated from my last job?

But honestly, it wasn't just fear holding me back. The pandemic had been a wake-up call, reminding me how short and unpredictable life could be. Like so many others, I found myself questioning what really mattered and whether the corporate grind was worth the personal cost. I was burned out—not just from the long hours and constant pressure, but also from navigating corporate politics and witnessing how businesses responded to unprecedented challenges. My values were tested in ways I hadn't expected, and I realized I wanted more meaning, autonomy, and alignment in my work and life.

I needed to discover what career move I wanted to make next. I needed to ensure it aligned with my natural strengths, gifts, talents, and zone of genius, and that it matched my financial and lifestyle goals. I needed to figure out what my zone of genius truly was, who I was at the soul level, what my purpose was, what my passions were, and how I could earn a living doing something I loved that made an impact in the world. How was I supposed to figure it all out?

As a reminder, your **challenge** is the problem or obstacle you're facing—the thing that's standing in your way or causing friction. Your **objective** is the specific outcome you want to achieve—the vision of success you're working toward.

Example (mine):
Challenge: I didn't know what the next phase of my career should be. I felt lost and uncertain about my direction, unclear if I wanted to continue down the marketing path yet unsure what kind of job outside of marketing and communication would be the right fit for me, and worried about how to find work that would provide both financial security and personal fulfillment.

Objective: To design a life and career I love that is aligned with a new high-vibe, abundant version of myself.

Example (client):
Challenge: I want to shift careers but feel limited by my degree and experience. I'm open to new opportunities but unsure which roles align with my skills without a significant pay cut or how to confidently market myself in a new field.

Objective: I want to find a fulfilling career path that motivates me and aligns with my values. I want financial security without feeling like I'm selling my soul.

Think of your challenge as the "problem statement" and your objective as the "goal statement." The clearer you are about what's standing in your way, the easier it is to define what success looks like on the other side.

CALL TO ACTION

IF YOU HAVE **THE REBRAND YOU COMPANION WORKBOOK,** HEAD TO THE SECTION OF THE CORRESPONDING CHAPTER AND COMPLETE THE ASSOCIATED QUESTIONS AND PROMPTS.

Reflection is the first step in rebranding your life. Ready to begin? Here's how to get started:

1. Carve out quiet time.
Find a distraction-free space where you can reflect without interruptions.

2. Gather your tools.
Grab the *Rebrand YOU Companion Workbook* at RebrandYouBook.com (visit the Resources section for more on the workbook and how to access it). You can totally complete all of the exercises in this book without it, but if you're like me and you like things streamlined, aggregated, and organized, I'd highly recommend getting the companion workbook as a complement to this book.

If the workbook isn't your thing, no worries. Create a Word Doc, Google Doc, or whatever digital tool helps you organize your thoughts. You can even kick it old school and handwrite in a journal or notebook. The key is to save your work in a place where you can easily reference it and add to it throughout your journey.

Pro Tip: While I love handwriting things, I would strongly suggest keeping a digital version—even if that means you type out what you wrote in your physical journal or notebook. The reason I'm suggesting digital is that it'll make it easier to repurpose your responses later in the book for other exercises (think: copy/paste).

3. Set up your system.
Create a folder on your computer titled "Rebrand You." Make a subfolder titled "Self-Assessment" for your upcoming exercises and notes.

4. Start reflecting.
Use the *Rebrand YOU Companion Workbook* or your chosen method of documentation to answer the following questions honestly:

- What is the biggest priority in your life right now?

- What is currently your biggest challenge?

- What is taking up most of your time and energy these days?

- How do you feel about how you're living today, both personally and professionally?

- What do you want to change, and why?

5. Write it down.
Take a moment to write down your answers. Be honest with yourself. This is your chance to get real, uncover the truth about where you are, and set a clear intention for where you want to go next.

If you're not exactly sure where you want to "go" yet, per se, that's OK. Don't worry about that logical left-brain right now.

Focus on how you're feeling now versus how you want to feel. The goal is to get clear on where you're experiencing friction or challenges and what your ideal end-state looks like.

6. Define your statements.
Fill in the blanks:
My Challenge Is: _____
My Objective Is: _____

When you're clear on your challenge and objective, you'll be ready to advance to the next phase: market research! This phase is critical because it will set things up for what comes next for you. You've got this! Taking the time to reflect is a powerful first step toward designing a life you love. When you've completed these steps, head over to Chapter 2: Self-Assessment Tools and Exercises.

CHAPTER 2

Self-Assessment Tools and Exercises

As a marketer, before launching any successful campaign, you first get clear on two things: the problem you're trying to solve (the challenge) and the *result* you want to achieve (the objective); and that's exactly what you just did in the last chapter. Go you!

Once you've defined those, the next step is market research, which involves gathering data, analyzing trends, and uncovering insights that will guide your strategy. Before kicking off any new marketing campaign, you need to understand the macro- and micro-level environment you're in.

In this step, we're going to go deeper into uncovering the truth of who you are and where you are. Self-assessment is one of the most powerful tools you can use to take the challenge and objective that you established in the last chapter even deeper.

In marketing, the market research phase is all about uncovering the cold, hard facts. We want to understand what's true about the past and present and what *could* be true about the future.

Market research is a critical and often rushed step in designing an effective campaign. So, to avoid that, right now I need you to set an intention of giving yourself permission to spend an adequate amount of time and not rushing to complete these exercises. They are foundational for unlocking areas of your life that may be keeping you stuck and holding you back from overcoming your challenge and fulfilling your objective. This part is critical for all the work that comes next.

How Market Research and Self-Assessment Help You

Self-assessment tools can help you uncover your values, passions, strengths, and areas for growth. They give you the data you need to make informed decisions about your life and career.

Without this information, you're just guessing and winging it. You're making claims about your life and strategic decisions about your future that haven't been substantiated with data and evidence to support them. Your internal legal and compliance department is panicking right now and calling external counsel to step in because you're basically on the verge of a reputational disaster.

So, don't get it twisted: Self-assessment isn't about labeling yourself or putting yourself into a box. It's about gaining clarity and self-awareness so you can make choices that align with who you truly are and desires you've always had but may have tucked away because you went down a career path or chose a relationship that felt "good on paper" or was something you felt was "the right thing to do" or your parents wanted you to do, etc.

Self-assessment is about getting to know yourself on a deeper level. It's about asking questions like:

- What makes me unique?

- What do I love to talk about?

- What motivates me and fuels my energy?

♦ What are my strengths, and how am I using them?

These questions might seem simple, but they can reveal a lot about who you are and what you want.

"Until you make the unconscious conscious, it will direct your life, and you will call it fate."
—Carl Jung

We'll get into the juicy unconscious and conscious mindset stuff in Step 4, but to sum it up, self-assessment is the process of making the unconscious conscious. It's about going through a series of self-discovery questionnaires and looking at the results to help you uncover the patterns, beliefs, and behaviors that are shaping your life—so you can take control and create a future that feels authentic and fulfilling.

During my healing process, I started by asking myself a series of questions designed to understand my current situation, how I got here, whether I was happy, what my challenge was, what my objective was, what success looked like, what I wanted, etc. Basically, who am I, and why am I here?

My strategy was to collect as much data on myself and my situation from as many different sources as I could. So, I went down a rabbit hole of self-discovery. Personality assessments, enneagram, DISC, Myers-Briggs, Human Design, reviewing old performance reviews, studying my journal, figuring out moments I felt happy and in flow, notes from psychic readings. I even requested my grade school transcripts from kindergarten through high school! Yes, I am that psycho. OK, I'll be nice. Yes, I am that type A!

It may seem like overkill, but you'd be surprised at how out of touch with ourselves we can get living on autopilot for an extended period. So, consider: How well do you *really* know yourself? Often, we think we know who we are, but do we really? Taking the time to complete these assessments and this level of self-analysis is extremely insightful. By reflecting on your values, understanding your personality type, exploring what you like, what you're naturally good at—and more—unlocks a fresh perspective and new level of self-awareness based on your current life circumstances.

I'll get into more specific self-assessment tools in the following few sections. You'll likely have your own unique questions you'll want to uncover answers for during this part of the market research phase, but here are some questions that generally apply to most people:

- How did I get here?

- What's working in my life right now?

- What's not working?

- What are my core values, and am I living in alignment with them?

- What are my greatest strengths, and how am I using them?

- What are my biggest challenges, and what's holding me back?

A Favor and Disclaimer Before We Jump into Some of the Tools I Used

When I started this process of self-reflection, I knew I wanted to go deep. I wasn't just looking for surface-level insights—I wanted to uncover the patterns and themes that had been shaping my life for decades. To do that, I used a variety of tools, both traditional and unconventional. My goal was to identify where my purpose, passion, and profit could intersect in a way that enabled me to serve others while feeling a sense of freedom in how I spend my time.

Before I jump into the exact steps I took, I need a favor. Please keep an open mind. Some of the methods and sources I used are certainly NOT in the Fortune 1000's employee handbook. And guess what? The workplace—correction, the world is changing in so many ways. So, some of the things you may roll your eyes at now as being woo-woo will likely be revered as fact and science-backed in just a few years from now.

I love data, and I love information from all sources. I often tell people that I believe in nothing and everything at the same time. So, I included ALL the things. I was open to ALL the feedback. The larger the sample size, the higher the probability for statistical significance and a high confidence score, am I right?

So, can you do that for me? Can you please keep an open mind?

Thanks, I knew you could.

Self-Assessment Tools and Exercises

When I was rebuilding my life after being fired, I went all in on self-assessment. That process helped me reconnect with my authentic self and gave me the clarity I needed to move forward. It was one of the most eye-opening things I did. It reminded me of the things I had loved before life got complicated—things like writing, creativity, and helping others.

There are countless self-assessment tools and exercises out there, and each one offers a unique perspective on who you are and how you operate. Some focus on your personality, while others help you identify your values, strengths, or passions.

Here's a quick overview of some popular tools and exercises:

Personality Tests

Personality tests are a great starting point for self-assessment because they help you understand your core motivations, strengths, and how you interact with the world. Here are a few to consider:

- **Myers-Briggs Type Indicator (MBTI):** This test identifies your personality type based on how you perceive the world and make decisions. Are you an introvert or an extrovert? Do you rely on logic or intuition? The MBTI can help you understand how you process information and interact with others.

- **Enneagram:** The Enneagram explores your core motivations, fears, and desires. It identifies nine personality types, each with its own strengths and challenges. This tool is especially helpful for understanding your emotional patterns and how they influence your behavior.

- **DISC Assessment:** The DISC assessment focuses on your communication style and how you work with others. It's often used in professional settings to improve teamwork and collaboration.

- **Human Design:** Human Design combines elements of astrology, the I Ching, and other systems to create a unique blueprint of your personality and energy. It's a more spiritual tool, but it can provide fascinating insights into how you're wired.

Values Exercises

Your values are the foundation of who you are. They guide your decisions, shape your priorities, and influence how you spend your time.

To identify your values, try this exercise:

1. Write down a list of ten to fifteen things that are most important to you. These could include things like family, freedom, creativity, health, or financial security.

2. Choose your top five values.

3. Reflect on how these values show up in your life. Can you think of a few ways you're incorporating them into your life? Are there things you're doing that go against your values? Think about how you are or are not living in alignment with your values, and if you're not, what needs to change?

Journaling

Do you journal? Journaling is one of the simplest and most effective ways to reflect on your life and gain clarity.

I highly recommend journaling as a form of releasing trapped energy and emotions from your body at a cellular level. You can just channel whatever thoughts come into your mind in free-form writing. I'll explain more about what that means later, but journaling is a form of energy clearing and can connect you to your higher self and be a beautiful guide for capturing key pieces of information and downloads that serve as little clues throughout your life. More on that later!

Anyway, if you don't have a current journal that you can flip through to uncover truths about yourself, no need for FOMO.

Here are some journaling prompts to get you started:

- What do I love to talk about?

- What makes me unique?

- What are my biggest fears, and how are they holding me back?

- What would I do if I weren't afraid of failing?

- How would I spend my time if money didn't matter?

- Where do I see myself in five years? Ten years?

Easier said than done, but setting aside ten to fifteen minutes each day to journal your thoughts is a freaking game-changer. Don't worry about grammar or structure. Just let your thoughts flow. It feels so good, and I can't tell you how amazing it is having a historical record of the activities in your daily life. This could be your big picture hopes and dreams, how you're feeling that day, what you ate for breakfast—it can be anything. Just let your thoughts flow without judgment.

Even before these three traumatic events, by looking at old journal entries, I was able to unlock critical pieces of information that helped me validate things I was feeling or thinking about doing. Looking at old journal entries helped me make the decision to sell my house in Pittsburgh, Pennsylvania, end my engagement, and start a fresh version of my life in Scottsdale, Arizona—just me and my two dogs.

My past journal entries helped me see how that decision was aligned with the type of lifestyle I was looking for. The journal entries made me feel confident that I could bet on myself and that the payoff would likely be greater than the fear. I could see that I had to embrace the unknown instead of staying in a familiar place and my comfort zone. Spoiler alert: I was right. I've been living happily in Arizona since 2014.

Career-Specific Questions

If you're reflecting on your career, these questions can help you gain clarity about what's working and what's not:

- What is your current job role, and what made you take the job?

- What are three things you love about your current job and three things you want to change?

- What is your goal salary?

- Think about a recent high point at work. What emotions did you feel in that moment? What about a recent low point—what emotions came up for you then?

- When you imagine your ideal workday, what feelings do you want to experience most often?

- What contribution do you hope your work makes to your team, your company, or even to society at large?

- If you could be remembered for one thing in your professional life, what would it be?

- Are there any values or causes you wish you could support more through your work?

- When you leave a job or project, what do you hope people will say about your impact?

- What's one thing you wish you had the courage to try in your career but haven't yet?

- Who is a business leader (or leaders) you're inspired by, and why?

These questions can help you identify what you want to change in your career and what steps you need to take to get there.

Zone of Genius

The "zone of genius" is where your work aligns with your unique talents, passions, and strengths, leading to effortless flow and deep fulfillment.

Essentially, it's the area where you are uniquely gifted and find the most joy and satisfaction in your work.

Here are some suggestions on how you can find yours:

Skills Inventory and Strengths Assessments

- List what you're naturally good at: Write down your core strengths, technical skills, and any talents you possess.

- Consider assessments: Tools like the StrengthsFinder or other personality assessments can help you identify your innate talents.

- Notice what others come to you for: Are you the go-to person for brainstorming, troubleshooting, or calming chaos? That's a clue.

- Track your easy wins: What do you accomplish with minimal effort that others find challenging? (Yes, your superpowers count—even if you think *everyone can do that*.)

- Reflect on your learning curve: Which skills or tasks did you pick up quickly, even when you were new? Sometimes your strengths are hiding in plain sight.

Identifying Your Passions

- What genuinely excites you? What activities or topics make you lose track of time?

- Connect passions to your work: How can you incorporate your passions into your daily tasks or career path?

- Pay attention to what you nerd out about: What do you research for fun, talk about at parties, or get a little too enthusiastic about?

- Notice your energy levels: Which activities leave you feeling energized, not drained? (Hint: Your passions usually give you a boost, not burnout.)

- Recall childhood interests: What did you love doing before the world told you to "be realistic"? Sometimes your inner kid knows best.

Reflecting on Past Successes

- Remember what felt easy and enjoyable: What projects or tasks have you consistently excelled at and enjoyed?

- Analyze what drove those successes: What specific skills, talents, and approaches contributed to your achievements?

- Identify your highlight reel: What are the moments you're most proud of in your career or life? What made them stand out?

- Look for patterns: Are there common threads in your wins—like teamwork, creativity, or problem-solving?

- Consider feedback from those moments: Did others recognize your contributions or celebrate your role? Sometimes, outside validation highlights what you do best.

Seeking Feedback

- Ask trusted colleagues or mentors: What do they perceive as your strongest abilities and areas of expertise?

- Use feedback to validate your self-assessment: Does their feedback align with your own insights about your strengths?

- Request specific examples: Ask people to share stories or situations where you made a difference—details make the feedback more actionable.

- Be open to surprises: Sometimes, others see strengths in you that you overlook or undervalue. (Yes, you really are *that* good at *[insert thing you always brush off]*.)

- Gather feedback from different sources: Don't just stick to work—ask friends, family, or even clients. Your strengths show up in all areas of life.

How to Use These Tools Effectively

Self-assessment tools are only as valuable as the effort you put into them. Here are some tips for getting the most out of these exercises:

1. **Be Honest with Yourself**

   - The more honest you are, the more accurate and helpful your results will be. Don't answer based on who you think you should be—answer based on who you truly are.

2. **Focus on the Process, Not Perfection**

   - Self-assessment is about exploration, not perfection. You don't need to have all the answers right away. The goal is to start uncovering insights about yourself, one step at a time.

3. **Don't Worry About Patterns Yet**

   - You might notice some patterns or themes as you go through these exercises, but don't stress about identifying them just yet. We'll dive deep into spotting patterns and analyzing your findings in Step 2: Examine and Analyze Your Findings. For now, focus on gathering as much information as you can about yourself. Think of this as your data collection phase.

4. **Give Yourself Grace**

- Self-assessment can bring up a lot of emotions, especially if you realize you've been living out of alignment with your true self. Be kind to yourself during this process and remember that self-awareness is the first step toward positive change.

Remember, self-assessment is a process. You don't have to figure everything out all at once. The goal is to gain clarity and self-awareness so you can take the next step in your journey with confidence.

CALL TO ACTION

IF YOU HAVE **THE REBRAND YOU COMPANION WORKBOOK,** HEAD TO THE SECTION OF THE CORRESPONDING CHAPTER AND COMPLETE THE ASSOCIATED QUESTIONS AND PROMPTS.

Here's what you're going to do next:
1. Head to the section in the *Rebrand YOU Companion Workbook* titled Chapter 2: Self-Assessment Tools and Exercises. All prompts and questions from this chapter, as well as direct links to the personality tests, are there for you to complete. Complete the assessments, note your results in the workbook, and save your work.

If you didn't purchase the *Rebrand YOU Companion Workbook,* follow these steps:

    2. Search online for each of the self-assessment tools I suggested. There are free versions of each of them.

    3. Give yourself enough time to complete each one. Consider blocking off time on your calendar.

    4. Create a folder on your computer titled "Self-Assessment" and save the results for each individual assessment in that folder.

    5. Create a new Google Doc or Word Doc and write out your answers to the values, questions, and journaling prompts I mentioned. Save the document in that same folder.

    6. Save your responses and assessment results and bookmark the file path to your Self-Assessment folder because we're going to be adding more to it and will be referring to it in Step 2 of the REBRAND Framework when we examine and analyze your findings.

Take your time and have fun with the assessments. In the next chapter, we'll focus on gathering feedback from others. Sometimes, others can spot patterns and strengths that we can't see in ourselves. This is an important part of the reflection process because it allows you to see yourself through the eyes of the people who know you best.

I'll see you in Chapter 3: Gathering Feedback from Others, where we'll explore how to ask for and use feedback to gain deeper insights into your current state.

CHAPTER 3

Gathering Feedback from Others

We've spent the last few chapters diving deep into self-reflection—exploring your values, passions, and limiting beliefs. But no matter how honest we are with ourselves, it's impossible to see the whole picture on our own.

The same goes for brands. Marketing folks are always seeking feedback on how our company's or clients' brands are perceived by internal and external stakeholders—e.g., employees, clients, customers, media, etc. We don't just rely on our own opinions; we conduct research to gather insights from each of our target stakeholder groups.

We use tools like surveys, focus groups, and social listening to understand metrics such as your favorability, credibility, market sentiment, and how likely people are to recommend you. We want to understand how our brand is perceived compared to competitors. We look at Key Performance Indicators (KPIs) to identify areas for improvement or to further differentiate and identify "white space" opportunities—i.e., gaps that few companies are solving for that we could pursue to capture market share.

The point is, we all have blind spots and areas where we're not aware of our own strengths, weaknesses, or patterns of behavior.

That's why gathering feedback from others is such a crucial part of the reflection process. It allows you to see yourself through the eyes of the people who know you best. It can reveal hidden strengths you didn't know you had as well as areas where you might be holding yourself back.

In the same way, gathering feedback about yourself is like conducting a qualitative and quantitative analysis of your personal brand. It helps you establish a baseline for how others perceive you, so you can identify what's working, what's not, and where you need to focus your efforts to move the needle in the right direction (once you know which direction is right for you, which the REBRAND Framework will help you figure out).

Seeing yourself through other people's eyes isn't always easy. In fact, it can feel downright vulnerable, like standing under a spotlight in your underwear. Sometimes, the feedback you get isn't what you hoped for, and that can sting. But being open to honest input is one of the bravest things you can do for yourself. If you're willing to be open and receptive, the insights you gain can be invaluable.

How External Feedback Can Help You

In marketing, understanding your brand's current state is essential for creating a successful campaign and refreshing your brand. You need to know where you stand before you can set goals and measure progress. The same is true for your personal growth. Gathering feedback from others can help you:

- **Identify Your Strengths and Weaknesses:** Just like a brand audit reveals what's working and what's not, feedback from others can help you understand your personal strengths and areas for improvement.

- **Gain a New Perspective:** Marketers use tools like Net Promoter Score (NPS) and sentiment analysis to understand how their audience feels about their brand. Similarly, feedback from others can help you see yourself from a fresh perspective and uncover blind spots.

- **Improve Your Communication Style:** In marketing, how you communicate your message can make or break your campaign. The same is true in life. Feedback on your communication style can help you identify areas where you might be misunderstood or ineffective.

- **Strengthen Your Relationships:** Asking for feedback shows others that you value their opinions and that you're committed to personal growth. This can strengthen your relationships and create deeper connections.

Who to Ask for Feedback

In marketing, you wouldn't ask just anyone for feedback on your brand—you'd target your ideal audience and key stakeholder groups. The same principle applies when gathering feedback about yourself. The key is to ask the right people.

When choosing who to ask for feedback, look for people who:

- **Know You Well:** The more familiar someone is with your personality, values, and goals, the more valuable their feedback will be.

- **Are Honest and Direct:** You want people who will tell you the truth, even if it's not what you want to hear.

- **Are Supportive and Constructive:** Look for people who will offer feedback in a way that's helpful and encouraging, not critical or judgmental.

Here are some potential sources:

- **Friends:** Friends who know you well can provide honest and supportive feedback on your personality, strengths, and weaknesses.

- **Family:** Family members can offer unique insights based on their long-term relationship with you. However, it's important to choose family members who can be objective and constructive.

- **Colleagues:** Colleagues can provide valuable feedback on your work ethic, communication style, and professional skills.

- **Mentors:** Mentors can offer guidance and support based on their own experiences and expertise.

- **Former Bosses/Supervisors:** These individuals can reflect on your work performance, strengths, and areas for improvement.

How to Ask Others for Input

Asking for feedback is like conducting a focus group or survey for your personal brand. You want to create an environment where people feel comfortable sharing their honest opinions. Here are some tips for making the process easier:

- **Be Clear About What You're Looking For:** Explain why you're asking for feedback and what you hope to gain from it. This will help people understand what kind of feedback would be most helpful.

- **Be Specific:** Instead of asking general questions like "What do you think of me?" ask specific questions about your strengths, weaknesses, communication style, or career goals.

- **Be Open-ended:** Avoid questions that can be answered with a simple yes or no. Instead, ask open-ended questions that encourage people to share their thoughts and feelings. For example:

  - When you think about my personal or professional strengths, what specific skills or qualities come to mind that you've seen me consistently demonstrate?

  - If you were to give me one piece of advice for my career growth or personal development, what would it be and why?

- **Create a Safe Environment:** Let people know that you're open to hearing honest feedback, even if it's not what you want to hear. Assure them that you won't get defensive or take their feedback personally.

- **Be Respectful of Their Time:** Acknowledge that they are doing you a favor by providing feedback. Be mindful of their time and schedule.

Types of Questions to Ask

Here are some examples of questions you can ask when gathering feedback:

About Your Strengths and Weaknesses

- What do you think are my greatest strengths?

- What are some areas where I could improve?

- What do you think I'm really good at?

- What do you think I struggle with?

About Your Communication Style

- How would you describe my communication style?

- How would you rate or describe my ability to listen?

- How would you rate or describe my ability to communicate my ideas clearly and effectively?

- Is there anything I could do to improve my communication skills?

About Your Personal Brand

- What three words would you use to describe me?

- What do you think I'm most passionate about?

- What do you think makes me unique?

- What do you think I stand for?

About Your Career Goals

- What do you think I'm best suited to do?

- What kind of career do you think would be a good fit for me?

- What skills or experiences do you think I need to develop?

- What do you think are my greatest career assets?

How to Receive Feedback

Receiving feedback is like analyzing a brand sentiment report—a document that gathers and summarizes what people are saying about a brand. You will likely find a mix of positive, neutral, and negative sentiment. And, of course, you always hope the negative sentiment is minimal!

Monitoring those reports can be so frustrating when you dig deep and read the consumer or user comments that are negative. You can get defensive, angry, and accusatory.

"How on Earth could they think THAT about ME? They have it all wrong. This must be a mistake!"

You might not like everything you hear, but the information is invaluable.

It's so important to approach this process with an open mind and a willingness to learn. As I learned during my NLP training, you can think you are the most effective communicator in the world. You can believe you have the most articulate, well-outlined, well-delivered message. But here's the kicker: Just because you think you nailed it doesn't mean the other person received it that way. If the person on the receiving end didn't interpret your message as you intended—if they applied their own meaning, misunderstood, or it caused conflict for them—then, I'm so sorry to inform you, but ...

... wait for it ...

You. Are. Not. An. Effective. Communicator.

The number one metric is whether they received and interpreted the message as you intended.

Don't get too hung up on this part right now because we'll be diving into communication delivery and rapport in detail later on, but remember that the way we want to be perceived isn't always how we are *actually* perceived. And there are lots of reasons why that is.

So for now, let's get back to making sure you've got some thick skin (go ahead, you can pinch yourself if you want to check). Good for you for taking all your collagen supplements and thickening up that skin, my friend!

Here are some tips for receiving feedback gracefully:

- **Listen Without Interrupting:** Let the person finish speaking before you respond. Avoid the temptation to interrupt or defend yourself if you're receiving feedback in a live environment, either in-person, over the phone, or via a web conferencing tool like Zoom.

- **Ask Clarifying Questions:** If you don't understand something, ask. This will help you make sure you're getting the full picture.

- **Express Gratitude:** Thank the person for taking the time to provide feedback. Let them know that you appreciate their honesty and their willingness to help you grow.

- **Don't Take It Personally:** Remember that feedback is about your behavior, not your worth as a person. Try to separate the feedback from your emotions and focus on what you can learn.

- **Take Time to Process:** Don't feel like you have to respond to the feedback immediately. Take some time to process what you've heard and decide how you want to use it.

What to Do with the Feedback After It's Received

The entire next section is all about examining and aggregating all the feedback and the research from the previous chapters. But because you're an overachiever, I know you want at least a little taste of what to do next. OK, I see you. You're my people. I won't leave you hanging.

Once you've gathered feedback from others, you'll need to make sense of it. So, some of the steps we'll discuss next will include:

- **Identify Patterns and Themes:** Look for common threads in the feedback you've received. Are there certain strengths or weaknesses that multiple people have mentioned?

- **Prioritize the Feedback That Resonates Most with You:** You don't have to act on every piece of feedback you receive. Focus on the feedback that feels most true and relevant to your goals.

- **Create an Action Plan:** Based on the feedback you've received, create a plan for how you're going to use it to improve. What specific steps can you take to build on your strengths and address your weaknesses?

- **Follow Up with the People Who Gave You Feedback:** Let them know how you're using their feedback and thank them again for their help. This will show them that you value their input and that you're committed to personal growth.

But don't worry about diving into these steps just yet! We're going to pull all of your feedback and market research together in Step 2 of the REBRAND Framework, when we examine and analyze your findings. For now, just focus on collecting your feedback and let yourself sit with it. We'll make sense of it soon.

CALL TO ACTION

IF YOU HAVE *THE REBRAND YOU COMPANION WORKBOOK,* HEAD TO THE SECTION OF THE CORRESPONDING CHAPTER AND COMPLETE THE ASSOCIATED QUESTIONS AND PROMPTS.

Identify three to five people you can ask for feedback. Use the questions in this chapter to guide your conversations, and be open to hearing what they have to say. Remember, feedback is a gift—even when it's not what you want to hear.

1. Complete this section in your *Rebrand YOU Companion Workbook,* or create a new Google Doc, Word Doc, or add a new section to one from the previous chapters, and title the document or section "Feedback from Others."

2. Review any past documentation that includes feedback from others, such as performance reviews or your saved emails from colleagues, clients, and partners.

3. Identify three to five (qualified) people you can ask for feedback now.

4. Schedule a phone or web conferencing call with your qualified peeps and ask them the suggested questions from this chapter and any other open-ended questions you'd like to include. You could also create a survey with a free tool like Google Forms with the questions, and email it to them, asking them to complete it by a specific deadline.

5. Save the responses from each person in the Self-Assessment folder that you bookmarked. We'll be referring to it in Step 2 of the REBRAND Framework. OK, we're done with collecting data! That was a lot, but so worth it. I promise.

In the next section, we'll start to examine and analyze all the information you've gathered. We're going to be looking for patterns and themes, identifying your strengths and weaknesses, and uncovering what's been holding you back.

Bust out your magnifying glass, Inspector Gadget. Because we're about to solve this case in Chapter 4: Spotting Patterns and Themes. (Props to the Old Millennials and Gen Xers who got the Inspector G reference.)

STEP 2

R

Examine and Analyze Your Findings

B

R

A

N

D

CHAPTER 4

Spotting Patterns and Themes

Congrats on making it to Step 2!

When marketers launch a campaign or a brand, they don't just throw ideas at the wall and hope something sticks. They analyze data to uncover patterns and trends that reveal what's working, what's not, and where they should focus their efforts. They look for insights that will help them create a brand or campaign that resonates with their audience and achieves their goals.

You've spent the last few chapters gathering data about yourself—exploring your values, passions, competencies, and feedback from others. Now, it's time to analyze that data and look for patterns and themes.

It's now time to make sense of all the information you've gathered and create a cohesive picture of who you are. This is where we reveal your strengths, weaknesses, and opportunities for growth, which will help you draft a strategy for overcoming the challenges and achieving the objectives and goals you stated in Chapter 1.

Spotting patterns and themes is like **finding the story in the data.** Another way to describe this is finding the through line. A through line is a theme or message that runs consistently across different communication channels and touchpoints. This consistency helps create a cohesive brand identity and ensures that all communications reinforce the core message.

OK, time to nerd out on all the quantitative and qualitative data and inputs we gathered in the last section. I'm going to walk you through several data inputs I used, and then you'll learn how to use AI tools like ChatGPT to help you analyze and extract the key details that we'll use to create your own personal brand through line and central messaging themes. This information is critical for ideating on the tactical steps we're going to lay out in a strategic plan to achieve your objective.

I'm going to be vulnerable and share with you the juicy details of what I discovered about myself, so you can get an idea of what you can uncover when you analyze the data about *yourself*.

Also, remember, you promised you'd keep an open mind? Good, because I'm about to get a little woo-woo on you. And yeah, I know what some of you might be thinking: *Oh, for Christ's sake, here we go with the crystals and manifesting.* But hold up! If you feel your inner skeptic twitching, just roll your eyes, take a deep breath, and stick with me. I promise, it's cool stuff—and science-y. Now that that's out of the way, here's a refresher on my personal challenge and objective:

Challenge: I didn't know what the next phase of my career should be. I felt lost and uncertain about my direction, unsure what kind of job would be the right fit for me, and worried about how to find work that would provide both financial security and personal fulfillment.

Objective: To design a life I love that is aligned with a new high-vibe, abundant version of myself.

Like I said, I was open to using *anything* to help me understand how to solve this. Let's start with the weird one: grade school transcripts. Why? Because it was one of the most insightful artifacts and data inputs I gathered.

The $10 Grade School Transcripts

I know it sounds a little ridiculous, but I was curious to see if my childhood grades and activities could reveal anything about who I am today. So, I spent $10 to request my transcripts from my high school alma mater—and it was worth every penny.

As I flipped through the pages, I noticed patterns that validated what I already knew about myself. I was always strong in reading, writing, and social studies, and weaker in math and science.

I also saw how my extracurricular activities shifted over the years, reflecting the ups and downs of my personal life. For example, in sixth grade, I was a straight A student involved in cheerleading, ski club, Girl Scouts, chorus, track club, and intramural sports. But by eighth and ninth grade, my grades dropped, and I stopped participating in activities. Looking back, I realized this was the period when I started struggling with shame, body image, and self-worth. These were triggered by negative experiences compounded with a few choice comments from other kids about my mom's lifestyle and financial status, a broken heart from being dumped by my first love, and a few other instances and secrets that were exposed.

The first time I smoked pot was after finding a bag of weed inside my mom's purse. The purse hung from a hook on the back of her closet door—a cheap hollow wooden door with a shirtless poster of eighties heartthrob Billy Hufsey taped to the front. We lived in an upstairs duplex apartment—another thing I was ashamed of. I'd have kids climb the tree to get to my bedroom and not let them walk through my house, so they'd think we lived in the WHOLE house—not just half. Maybe you NYC and urban-dwelling natives can't relate, but where I grew up, none of my friends lived in an apartment in our small rural Western Pennsylvania town. Everyone I knew lived in a whole house, not just a section of one.

I was thriving when I could keep certain parts of my life veiled, but once my secrets were exposed and I was exposed to alcohol and drugs in middle school, my sense of self-worth plummeted along with my grades.

After school let out for summer at the end of my seventh-grade school year, I started hanging out with the skaters and older kids, I dropped out of cheerleading, and I started listening to Marilyn Manson.

When the eighth-grade school year kicked off, I showed up on the first day under my new brand: party girl who would ditch school and take hits of acid during the school day. I wore combat boots and dark eye makeup, giving zero fucks about academic achievements, and ready to fight anyone who dared say a bad thing about me, my family, or my cool new older friends.

This is a rebrand I am NOT proud of by any means.

Luckily, a teacher who knew me when I was in elementary school, where she taught before transferring to my middle school, pulled me aside and asked me what the hell I was doing. She knew me as the kid who volunteered to be the emcee for the elementary school talent show; I was a hype girl from the start, and she knew it. When I was in elementary school, Mrs. Eicher ran the school-wide talent show, and rather than perform a talent act, I tried out for the role of emcee. So, I got to announce the talent acts coming onto stage (interesting considering being an emcee is something I absolutely love doing now and look forward to expanding my role as hype-host and speaker).

I wasn't ready to let go of my new brand yet, but her words did sink in. And she suggested I join the Mass Media Club and try out for the school play she was leading. I think I took her up on her offer more out of sarcasm, but little did I know, I was really freaking good at acting and doing the school announcements.

Luckily, the Marilyn Manson phase only lasted for one season. After a couple more years of trauma, car accidents, friends overdosing, school suspensions, arrests, and probation later, my high school homeroom teacher, Mr. B, pulled me aside and asked me what the hell I was doing.

He was right. This wasn't me.

It was time for a rebrand.

By the time my junior year of high school started, I had already transformed. I was hyperfocused on academics, school clubs, and ensuring my final two years of high school were college-application worthy because I knew education was my ticket out of repeating generational patterns.

Another key event happened that propelled my transformation: My mom ditched her loser boyfriend, who was the culprit of so much trauma we experienced (which I'm still healing from today). After Loser, she began dating an amazing man who was one of the most influential adults in my life during my formidable high school and college years (and still is to this day).

I call him my Dad-Dad because while he's not my biological father, he has been a consistent father figure and positive male influence in my life for over twenty-five years. He retired from a good white collar job in the nuclear engineering field and helped me acclimate to a world outside of my small hometown culture.

That positive rebrand shaped my identity leading into early adulthood. When I turned eighteen, I knew that if I ever got arrested again, it would go on my permanent record and ruin any chance I'd have of achieving my full potential. And with barely any money to afford college, I couldn't risk having the fines to pay since I could barely afford tuition, books, and living expenses.

I never did get arrested again, THANK GOD, and I've been largely embodying a "good girl" persona ever since (more on that later).

Seeing these patterns in black and white was a powerful reminder of how much I've grown and how my past has shaped who I am today. It also reinforced the importance of reflecting on where I've been to understand where I'm going. By looking at my transcripts, I was able to validate what I intuitively knew I've always been good at, interested in, and naturally gifted at. Why not give it a try and request YOUR grade school transcripts? Take a walk down memory lane and see what you uncover, my friend!

Personality Test Assessment Data

As you embark on your self-discovery journey, consider exploring various personality assessments. They're fun (at least I think they are!) and a fantastic form of personal market research.

I took several personality tests to help me understand my preferences, inherent traits, strengths, weaknesses, and preferred ways of living and interacting with other people to see if my career path was in line with my natural, God-given state of being.

Tools like DISC, MBTI, Enneagram, and Human Design can offer incredible insights. (These are the ones I used, and I explain them each individually below.) There are many more assessment tools outside of these, so if you want to use others too, go for it! My position is that the more data you have, the better the analysis and output.

Many of these systems, such as Human Design, offer free basic chart generation online, allowing you to dive right in. For others—like DISC, MBTI, and the more in-depth Enneagram assessments—the official, validated versions are typically paid. The good news is that there are also many free online quizzes and resources available that can provide a wonderful starting point for your exploration. These can be a fun and insightful way to begin understanding yourself through these frameworks. If you find yourself resonating with a particular system and are in a position to invest, pursuing the official, validated assessments or working with a certified practitioner can offer even richer, more nuanced insights.

Remember, these are just a few of the many powerful self-assessment tools out there. Trust your intuition and explore what resonates most with you and your unique journey. The goal is to find what helps you understand yourself better and move forward with clarity and confidence.

I'm going to share my results and their interpretation with you so you can see how robust and helpful the information can be to illuminate different aspects of your inner world and unique makeup.

DISC Assessment

The DISC assessment[4] is a personality test that measures four behavioral traits: Dominance (D), Influence (I), Steadiness (S), and Conscientiousness (C). It's often used in professional settings to improve communication, teamwork, and leadership.

My Results: Strong I Personality (with a Hint of D)

- **I (Influence):** Enthusiastic, persuasive, sociable, and optimistic. People with a strong I personality excel at building relationships, inspiring others, and creating a positive atmosphere.

- **Hint of D (Dominance):** Goal-oriented, decisive, and driven. The D trait adds a layer of assertiveness and ambition to my personality.

What This Means for Me:
I'm a natural communicator and motivator. I thrive in roles where I can connect with people, share ideas, and inspire action. The D in my

---

4 Everything DiSC®, "What Is the DiSC Model," accessed August 3, 2025, https://www.everythingdisc.com/what-is-disc.

profile gives me the drive to take charge and make things happen, which has been a key factor in my success as a leader and strategist.

This insight affirmed that I should continue to lean into my ambition and opportunities that enable me to build relationships with people, bring good vibes and energy, assume a leadership role, and inspire my clients and teams to believe in themselves and our ability to achieve our desired goals and the KPIs we want to hit.

Myers-Briggs Type Indicator (MBTI)

The MBTI is a personality test that categorizes people into sixteen types based on how they perceive the world and make decisions.[5] It's widely used for personal development and career planning.

My Results: ENFJ (The Protagonist/Teacher)

- **Core Traits:** Charismatic, altruistic, organized, and inspiring. ENFJs are natural leaders who are deeply empathetic and driven to help others grow.

- **Strengths:** ENFJs excel at building relationships, motivating others, and creating a vision for the future. They are often described as Givers who prioritize the well-being of others.

What This Means for Me:
This absolutely is me at my core. As an ENFJ, I'm passionate about helping others unlock their potential. Whether I'm mentoring a col-

---

5 The Myers-Briggs Company, "MBTI," accessed August 3, 2025, https://www.themyersbriggs.com/en-US/Products-and-Services/Myers-Briggs.

league, coaching a client, or writing this book, my goal is always to inspire and empower. According to PsychCentral.com, ENFJs are a rare personality type and represent only about 2.5 percent of the total population[6].

This insight affirmed that I should continue to lean into opportunities that enable me to share my insights and help others learn and grow into their highest potential.

Human Design

Human Design is a system that combines astrology, the I Ching, Kabbalah, and the chakra system to provide a blueprint of your energy, purpose, and decision-making style. As explained in *The Definitive Book of Human Design* by Ra Uru Hu and Lynda Bunnell, the system offers practical insights into how we are wired to operate in the world, make decisions, and interact with others.[7]

My Results: 3/6 Manifesting Generator

- **3/6 Profile (Martyr/Role Model):** This profile is all about learning through trial and error. The first phase of life is about experimenting, making mistakes, and gaining wisdom through experience. After that, the 6-line steps into the role model phase, where you share the lessons you've learned and inspire others by living authentically.

---

6 Jenna Fletcher, "What Are the Rarest Personality Types?" Psych Central, August 26, 2023, accessed October 4, 2025, https://psychcentral.com/health/rarest-personality-type.

7 Ra Uru Hu and Lynda Bunnell, *The Definitive Book of Human Design: The Science of Differentiation* (Carlsbad, CA: Human Design Press, 2011), 15.

- **Manifesting Generator:** This energy type is known for being multipassionate, fast-moving, and efficient. Manifesting Generators are here to follow their passions, pivot when necessary, and show others that it's OK to change direction as you grow.

What This Means for Me:
I've always been someone who learns by doing. I've made mistakes, taken risks, and tried new things—and every experience has taught me something valuable. As a Manifesting Generator, I thrive when I'm juggling multiple passions and projects, which explains why I've had such a diverse career path. This insight has helped me embrace my nonlinear journey and see it as a strength rather than a weakness.

This insight affirmed that I should share the lessons I've learned throughout my life to inspire other people to live a life that feels authentic to them. I've made lots of mistakes along my journey, but that was all part of the divine plan because they happened FOR me. I need to learn things through trial and tribulation (often the hard way). What's most important is that I learn the lesson and embody the learning in the next phase—and help others take an easier path than I did by teaching what I've learned.

Enneagram

The Enneagram is a personality system that identifies nine core types—each with its own motivations, fears, and growth paths—and is widely regarded as a powerful tool for self-awareness and personal growth. Don Richard Riso and Russ Hudson—founders of The Enneagram Institute, the most widely recognized official source for the Enneagram in the English-speaking world—have written extensively on the system's depth and transformative potential.[8]

**My Results: My Results: 2w3
(The Helper with an Achiever Wing)…but also a 7**
When I initially took the Enneagram assessment a few years ago, my result was a type 7. However, a more recent assessment yielded a 2w3. It appears that Enneagram results can shift based on life circumstances, personal growth, and stress. To reconcile these findings, I consulted an AI model to help synthesize the two possible results.

My results reflect a blend of type 7 (The Enthusiast) and type 2w3 (The Helper with an Achiever Wing). As a type 7, I am adventurous, optimistic, and driven by a desire for freedom, variety, and avoiding pain. As a 2w3, I am empathetic, people-oriented, and motivated by a need to feel loved and valued, with the three-wing adding ambition, charm, and a focus on achievement. This combination suggests I am both energetic and caring, with a magnetic personality that thrives on connection and excitement.

What This Means for Me:
This blend makes me a vibrant and compassionate individual who brings joy and care to others while pursuing new experiences. However, I may feel torn between my need for freedom (7) and my desire to be needed and admired (2w3), which can lead to overcommitting or burnout. To grow, I need to focus on balancing my adventurous spirit with meaningful relationships, set boundaries to avoid overextending myself, and embrace moments of discomfort to deepen my self-awareness and personal growth. This insight affirmed that the best type of

---

8 Don Richard Riso and Russ Hudson, *The Wisdom of the Enneagram: The Complete Guide to Psychological and Spiritual Growth for the Nine Personality Types* (New York: Bantam, 1999).

job for me would allow me to express my creativity, build meaningful relationships, and maintain a sense of excitement and purpose.

Astrology

Since I was a little girl, I loved reading my horoscope while in line at the supermarket with my mom. Astrology has always fascinated me, and as I started exploring my chart as an adult, it finally made sense why I never fully resonated with the straight-up Pisces sun sign horoscopes—because I'm a Cusp!

Cusps were born on a day within the transition period of two zodiac signs, which means they'll often have characteristics of both zodiac signs. When I read the description for Aquarius-Pisces Cusp, I felt so seen!

My Results: Aquarius-Pisces Cusp Sun, Gemini Moon, Libra Rising

Having my sun on the Aquarius-Pisces Cusp blends the intellectual, innovative energy of Aquarius with the intuitive, compassionate nature of Pisces. This makes me a visionary thinker with a deep emotional core, driven by a desire to make a meaningful impact. My Gemini moon adds mental agility, curiosity, and a love for communication, helping me process emotions through logic and thrive on variety. With Libra Rising, I exude charm, diplomacy, and a natural ability to connect with others, making me socially graceful and focused on creating harmony in my relationships.[9]

---

9 "Aquarius Sun, Pisces Moon, Libra Rising—Meaning," Astrology.com, accessed August 3, 2025, https://www.astrology.com/sun-moon-rising/aquarius-sun-pisces-moon-libra-rising.

What This Means for Me:
This astrological combination highlights my unique ability to balance intellect, emotion, and social connection. I am a creative and empathetic person who thrives on meaningful relationships, intellectual stimulation, and opportunities to express my visionary ideas. To grow, I focus on aligning my need for freedom and variety with my desire to help others and maintain harmony. I seek out environments that let me explore my creativity, connect deeply with others, and make a positive impact on the world.

These insights have affirmed that I need to pursue opportunities where I can express my creativity, build connections, and make a meaningful difference. I truly need variety, intellectual stimulation, and the chance to contribute to something larger than myself.

Psychic Readings

I was really going through it in 2018. It was a period of confusion after ending a relationship and feeling anxious about my job, so I reached out to a psychic that a friend recommended. Before I go further, I want to acknowledge that the world of psychics and intuitives is vast and not always trustworthy. There are many charlatans out there, so if you ever feel called to seek guidance, I strongly encourage you to go to someone who comes highly recommended by people you trust. I was seeking guidance to make sense of what was happening in my life.

In our first reading, the friend-recommended psychic told me that my life purpose involves a creative yet healing modality, likely tied to words and mental healing and helping others reach their potential. He told me this purpose will unfold in the coming years, requiring patience and surrender. After I got fired, I reached out to a different psychic (also recommended by a friend), and she told me there was a conspiracy surrounding my termination because someone was threatened by my light and rising influence. Don't shoot the messenger, I'm just letting you know what a psychic told me. (shrug emoji.) If that's true and the person (or people) responsible is reading this book right now, thank you so much, because now I get to shine my light with so many more people!

In the summer of 2024, I was feeling anxious again about my career path, so I scheduled a session with an intuitive woman who previously worked in global communications and had recently come out publicly with her additional skills beyond marketing and PR: an intuitive medium. She performed an Akashic records reading for me and connected with my spirit guides. In that session, she said these were my soul purpose and life purpose:

Soul Purpose: Enjoy the journey. Love is always the destination. You will teach along the way at every stop.

Life Purpose: Collect the lessons and teach what you have learned. Some are simple, some are complex. Love is at the center of them all. They will not land unless you love and trust yourself with these truths.

The insights from these readings helped me to see how my personal experiences, both the highs and the lows, seem to all be part of a bigger picture themed around teaching and helping people realize their gifts and potential.

Isn't that interesting, considering I'm now teaching you how to realize your gifts and potential in this book?

What I Love and Talk About

As I reflected on my results, I noticed that the things I love and talk about most align perfectly with my personality and purpose. Here's a snapshot of what lights me up:

- **Topics I'm Passionate About:** Neuroscience, marketing, education, life design, mindset, psychology, fitness, self-development, communication, relationships, dreams, aspirations, comedy, spirituality, and business

- **Activities I Love:** Skiing, paddleboarding, kayaking, bike riding, UTV riding, cooking, spending time with my dog, deep conversations, watching/listening to thought-provoking podcasts, connecting people, and exploring the mountains and water

These passions are a big part of who I am, and they've shaped the way I approach my work, my relationships, and my life.

Use AI to Help You Analyze Data, Spot Patterns, and Identify Themes

It may sound strange to use technology for something as personal as self-reflection, but like it or not, we are living in the digital age. One that is rapidly being transformed by artificial intelligence. So, it's no surprise that AI has found its way into the world of personal development.

For me, using AI was a helpful starting point. I began by feeding my self-assessment results, feedback from others, and personal reflections into ChatGPT and asked questions like:

- What patterns can you identify in this feedback?

- What are the recurring themes in my self-assessment results?

- What story is this data telling me?

Using AI felt a bit like having a personal assistant for my self-reflection process. The insights I gained were eye-opening and gave me a fresh perspective, along with several ideas for how I could introduce a rebranded me in real life.

AI helped me see that my passion for education and storytelling was a recurring theme across all my reflections, and it helped me organize my findings into clear categories, making it easier to spot patterns and connect the dots.

That said, it's important to acknowledge that while AI can be a useful tool for surfacing patterns and sparking new ideas, it does have its limitations. Technology can't replace the depth, nuance, and empathy that come from working with a real person who understands your unique context. For those who want to go deeper, get more personalized support, or navigate complex emotions and decisions, partnering with a trusted guide—someone who can listen, challenge, and encourage you—can make all the difference.

For me, the combination of AI insights and human guidance has been invaluable. My hope is that you'll use whatever tools are available to you, but also remember that real transformation often happens in relationship, with yourself and with others (real human beings, not tech!) who can support your growth. You'll learn more about the power of relationships in Chapter 16.

That mix of AI and human reflection didn't just give me clarity. It lit up the patterns I'd been circling for years, finally connecting the dots into something that made sense. These insights painted a clear picture of who I am: a natural leader, lifelong learner, teacher, and storyteller who thrives on connection, creativity, and helping others grow—either personally or in business.

My purpose is to use my experiences to help others design their own lives with intention and creativity. And my journey—every high, every low, every twist and turn—has prepared me to do just that.

Understanding my Manifesting Generator Human Design type brought so much relief and made me feel seen. I'd been trying so hard to figure things out and find my niche and narrow my focus to be known for one thing. But it's not in my design to pick just one thing. My gift is that I'm a multipassionate person. I have range and moxie, two adjectives an executive in my network used to describe me. As a

Manifesting Generator, I have the capacity for multiple things and to be able to master new subjects quickly.

So, my business today is a multidisciplinary consultancy because I'm skilled in and interested in a wide range of things. I can help people and businesses and add value in many ways, including marketing, communication, comedy, career coaching, business and culture transformation, life design, speaking, workshops, mindset, NLP, motivation, energy healing, and more.

CALL TO ACTION

IF YOU HAVE **THE REBRAND YOU COMPANION WORKBOOK,** HEAD TO THE SECTION OF THE CORRESPONDING CHAPTER AND COMPLETE THE ASSOCIATED QUESTIONS AND PROMPTS.

Complete this section in your *Rebrand YOU Companion Workbook*, or create a new Google Doc, Word Doc, or add a new section to one from the previous chapters, title the document or section "Examination and Analysis," and complete the steps and prompts below.

Remember that Self-Assessment folder and the document(s) I told you to save in it? We're going to use the data to connect the dots so you can begin to solve your challenge and objective—the area where you're feeling stuck, disempowered, and confused about what to do about it.

For me, the category where I felt stuck was my next career move. Maybe that's exactly what yours is, or perhaps it's your romantic relationship or your friendships, your health, or even your financial goals. This process is flexible and can be used to gain clarity in any area where you want to grow or make a change.

So, as you dive into your personal market research, you'll want to collect information that paints a broad picture of *you* as a whole *and* specific data that sheds light on the particular challenge you're tackling.

Depending on the area of your life you choose to focus on, you'll want to tailor your market research approach and the types of inputs you gather. For example, if you're exploring your health, you might include information from medical tests, fitness trackers, or wellness assessments. If you're focusing on finances, you could gather data like spending habits, savings goals, or financial statements. The key is to collect inputs that are most relevant to the area you want to understand and improve.

Here are the steps you're going to follow:

1. Gather All Your Inputs You Saved in Your Self-Assessment Folder

- Personality test results (e.g., DISC, MBTI, Enneagram, Human Design)

- Feedback from friends, family, colleagues, and mentors

- Notes from journaling or self-reflection exercises

- Performance reviews or professional evaluations

- Childhood memories, grade school transcripts, or old report cards

- Any other insights you've gathered, even if they seem unconventional (e.g., astrology charts, psychic readings, or intuitive insights)

2. Look for Recurring Themes
Now that you have all your data in one place, it's time to start analyzing it. Look for recurring themes, patterns, and insights. Here are some questions to guide you:

- What strengths or talents keep coming up?

- Are there any consistent weaknesses or challenges?

- What values or passions are mentioned repeatedly?

- Are there any surprising insights that stand out?

- How do your results align with your current life and career?

3. Use AI to Spot Patterns
Use an AI tool like ChatGPT to analyze your data and do the following:

- Take all the information you've gathered and organize it into one document or spreadsheet.

- Copy and paste that document into ChatGPT.

- Ask specific questions and prompts to help you identify patterns and themes.

Here are some prompts you can use:

- You are a top life, business, career, relationship, and financial coach and adviser with 20+ years of experience and the most advanced training in your field. The clients you've worked with are happy, healthy, financially, personally, and professionally successful, fulfilled, making an impact, and living their purpose and best lives. Analyze the following data and provide me with insights and direction so that I can also become as happy and fulfilled as your existing clients. I'd like you to address the questions below, but please also ask me any clarifying questions. *[Upload or copy/paste your assessment data.]*

  - What do my personality test results say about how I interact with others and approach challenges?

  - How can I use my strengths to overcome my weaknesses and achieve my goals?

  - What lessons can I learn from my past experiences to help me grow and move forward?

  - What patterns or themes can you identify in this data about my life experiences, strengths, and challenges?

  - How do my strengths, passions, and values align to create a cohesive personal brand?

  - What insights can I take away from this data to help me design a life that feels authentic and aligned?

4. Reflect on Your Findings

You should receive a summarization and analysis that addresses your prompt. Keep in mind that ChatGPT doesn't always get it right so you may need to revise your prompts, expand your questions, ask for clarification, etc.

Once you've identified the patterns and themes in your data, take some time to reflect on what they mean for you. This is something you shouldn't rely on AI for—it should come from your heart and intuition.

Here are some questions to guide your reflection:

- Did anything surprise you?

- Are your results aligned with how you're currently living?

- How do you want to be perceived by others?

- Did you identify any strengths or weaknesses?

By analyzing your patterns and themes, you're taking the first step toward clarity, alignment, and intentionality. You're reclaiming your power to make a significant change in your life so that you rebrand and design a life that feels true to you.

In Chapter 5: Conducting Your Personal SWOT, I'll walk you through how to create a SWOT analysis to uncover your strengths, weaknesses, opportunities, and threats as it relates to your challenge and objective.

Alexis Castorina

CHAPTER 5

Conducting Your Personal SWOT

Have you ever had to create a SWOT analysis at work or review one with your colleagues? The acronym SWOT stands for Strengths, Weaknesses, Opportunities, Threats.

I've created and used many o' SWOTs throughout my career. They always felt annoying, and I always had a difficult time putting things in the cookie-cutter quadrants because some things felt like they always overlapped (hello, Manifesting Generator type—can't choose one quadrant)! But, when finished, they were always extremely helpful and provided great direction on short- and long-term business planning, determining strategic priorities, and then how to rank them to determine what gets done first and why based on the unique scoring criteria you developed that makes sense to your business. I could write a whole book on THAT, but for now …guess what?

I figured out that just like businesses use a SWOT analysis, we can use it to inform the strategic priorities in our personal lives too!

A SWOT is a simple yet powerful framework that helps organizations identify internal and external factors that can impact their success. Here's a breakdown of each category:

- **Strengths:** Internal attributes that give the company a competitive advantage. These could include strong brand recognition, a loyal customer base, or innovative products, to name a few.

- **Weaknesses:** Internal attributes that put the company at a disadvantage. These might include limited resources, outdated technology, or gaps in the workforce.

- **Opportunities:** External factors that the company can capitalize on to grow or improve. Examples include emerging markets, new technologies, or changes in consumer behavior.

- **Threats:** External factors that could harm the company's success. These might include increased competition, economic downturns, or regulatory changes.

Marketing teams, corporate strategy teams, and executive leadership often use SWOT analyses to:

- Identify areas where the company is excelling and where it needs improvement.

- Develop short- and long-term strategies to address weaknesses and capitalize on opportunities.

- Anticipate potential threats and create contingency plans.

- Align the company's goals with its strengths and opportunities while mitigating risks.

For example, I've conducted a SWOT analysis for every brand I've worked with. This is a foundational analysis that should be done any time you join a new company or onboard a new client.

Why? Because you need to evaluate and establish a baseline of the brand's current position in the market. This is how you architect a strategy to achieve whatever primary business goals were established, i.e., the business challenge and objective. Remember Chapter 1?

For instance, if the brand's strength is its loyal customer base but its weakness is a lack of social media presence, the team might develop a strategy to improve its digital marketing efforts to increase brand awareness and reach.

Similarly, if an opportunity exists to expand into a new market to increase revenue, the team might prioritize expansion strategies into contextually related, parallel, or "sister" categories. (There are lots of other annoying buzz words and business jargon you could use for this same concept.)

The point is, you don't know where you're going, what possibilities exist, or what might get in your way until you know where you're at. You get the idea.

How to Conduct Your Personal SWOT Analysis

This classic tool from the business world is just as powerful when you use it to map out your own life and career.

Abruptly leaving my corporate job was scary, but I knew it was a huge blessing in disguise and an opportunity to reevaluate my career and life. I wanted to better understand my personal brand positioning and create a unique scorecard so I'd have criteria to evaluate what came next in my career and life.

I'll provide a general overview of what this could look like for you, and then I'll share a high-level overview of my SWOT. Don't spend a ton of time on this, because in the Call to Action section at the end of the chapter, I have specific prompts for you to dive into your own self-assessment.

Here's how you can approach it:
Strengths
Think about what you're naturally good at, the skills you've honed, and the qualities people compliment you on. These could be things like:

- Communication (writing, speaking, listening)
- Problem-solving or creative thinking
- Empathy and relationship building
- Technical expertise in your field
- Adaptability or resilience

Weaknesses
Be honest with yourself—where do you struggle, or what habits hold you back? Some examples:

- Procrastination or time management issues
- Difficulty saying no or setting boundaries
- Perfectionism or fear of making mistakes
- Struggling to delegate or ask for help
- Getting easily distracted or losing focus

Opportunities
Look for areas where you can grow, expand, or capitalize on new trends. Consider:

- New skills you want to learn or certifications to pursue

- Growing industries or emerging platforms

- Expanding your network or finding mentors

- Personal interests you could turn into a side hustle

- Changes in your life circumstances that open new doors

Threats
Identify the external factors or internal fears that could get in your way. For example:

- Economic uncertainty or job market shifts

- Burnout or health challenges

- Fear of failure or impostor syndrome

- Family or societal expectations

- Competition in your field

Here's what this looked like for me:
When I did my own personal SWOT analysis, I wanted to take a step back, establish a baseline of where I was, and figure out how I could intentionally design my dream life and the type of career that would align with my strengths, ideal day-to-day lifestyle, and goals I wanted to achieve before I died.

Strengths
- Strong communication skills (writing, speaking, and storytelling)
- Natural ability to connect with people and build relationships
- Creative thinker with a passion for education, marketing, comedy, neuroscience, and life design

Weaknesses
- Struggles with time management and perfectionism
- Tendency to overthink and second-guess decisions
- Difficulty delegating tasks and asking for help

Opportunities
- Growing interest in life design, neuroscience, and personal development
- Ability to leverage network and professional experience to build a personal brand
- Emerging platforms and tools can help scale impact

Threats
- Fear of failure and impostor syndrome
- Financial uncertainty with entrepreneurship
- External pressures and lifestyle expectations

This exercise was incredibly eye-opening. It helped me see where I was excelling, where I needed to improve, and where I had opportunities to grow. It also gave me clarity on the external challenges I needed to navigate.

Your strengths are the compass, guiding you toward opportunities that align with your talents and passions. When you know your strengths, you can leverage them to create a life and career that feel authentic and fulfilling. You can focus on activities that energize you, build confidence, and make a meaningful impact.

Your weaknesses are the map, showing you where you might need more help. When you acknowledge your weaknesses, you can address them in a way that supports your goals, whether that means seeking help, delegating tasks, or developing new skills.

It's not about becoming perfect or eliminating all your flaws. It's about understanding yourself deeply so you can make better decisions, leverage your talents, and create a life that feels aligned with who you truly are.

CALL TO ACTION

IF YOU HAVE *THE REBRAND YOU COMPANION WORKBOOK*, HEAD TO THE SECTION OF THE CORRESPONDING CHAPTER AND COMPLETE THE ASSOCIATED QUESTIONS AND PROMPTS.

Conduct a SWOT analysis on yourself. Follow the steps below and take time to reflect on your results.

Hey, stop! I can sense you're starting to feel overwhelmed. I get it, but don't because this won't take long—thanks to AI and the work you've already done and saved in your Assessment Data folder.

I'm going to make this super simple for you. OK, here we go.

1. Grab a sheet of paper and a pen, create a spreadsheet, or search for a SWOT template online. (Pinterest and Canva have really pretty templates you can use.)

If you're doing it from scratch on paper or a spreadsheet, create four quadrants and label them as follows:

STRENGTHS	**WEAKNESSES**
OPPORTUNITIES	**THREATS**

2. Next, we're going to use your assessment data and the results from the analysis you did in the last chapter as data inputs (also known as artifacts and evidence in corporate speak) to conduct your SWOT.

We want to uncover answers to these high-level questions (feel free to add more relevant questions of your own, if you'd like):

Strengths (upper left quadrant)
- -What are you naturally good at?
- -What skills, talents, or abilities set you apart?
- -What do others consistently compliment you on?

Weaknesses (upper right quadrant)
- -What areas do you struggle with?
- -What tasks or activities drain your energy?
- -What feedback have you received about areas for improvement?

Opportunities (lower left quadrant)
- -What trends or opportunities align with your strengths and passions?
- -What resources or tools are available to help you grow?
- -What connections or networks can you leverage?

Threats (lower right quadrant)
- -What external factors could hold you back?
- -What fears or limiting beliefs are getting in your way?
- -What challenges do you need to overcome?

You can use the prompts in the next section to help you get started, but feel free to modify and revise the questions/prompts as needed.

You can use an AI tool like ChatGPT, but doing it old school is perfectly fine too (and helps you exercise your critical thinking skills). And while AI is super helpful, convenient, and scarily accurate at times, it's not perfect, and results can vary based on how you're prompting the AI tool. Always be sure that you're going through and fact-checking AI, adding your own inputs, and thinking critically. Use your own discernment.

3. Prompts to Ask Yourself or AI

- **Yourself:** If you're doing this without the help of AI, use your critical thinking skills and objectively review your assessment results and any other factors you know to be true about your personal situation, and begin the process of inputting your responses into each SWOT quadrant.

- **AI:** You are a top life, business, career, relationship, and financial coach and adviser with 20+ years of experience and the most advanced training in your field. The clients you've worked with are happy, healthy, financially, personally, and professionally successful, fulfilled, making an impact, and living their purpose and best lives. I'd like to create a personal SWOT analysis to help me understand my strengths, weaknesses, opportunities, and threats as it relates to *[insert business challenge and objective]*. Analyze these assessment results *[insert results]* and create a four-quadrant SWOT analysis in a table format. Ask me any clarifying questions.

Spend as much time as you need on this SWOT. Save your results in your folder. When you're ready, I'll see you in the next section, where we'll explore how to leverage your strengths and opportunities and address your weaknesses and threats, which we will use as key data inputs for brainstorming concepts and then creating the strategy for your personal rebrand campaign.

STEP 3

R
E
Brainstorm Potential New Beginnings
R
A
N
D

CHAPTER 6

Envisioning Your Ideal Life

Congratulations, you made it to Step 3: Brainstorm Potential New Beginnings! This section is all about one of my favorite parts of the marketing campaign planning process: ideation and creative concepting!

So, before we jump into the tactical steps of brainstorming new ideas for your rebrand, I want you to get dreamy with me. Sounds fun, right?!

Close your eyes. Well, don't because you need to read first. Read, and then close your eyes: And remember when you were a kid. If you were anything like me, your imagination was always free-flowing and running wild.

This makes me think of the scene from one of my favorite nineties comedy movies, *Billy Madison,* where he was in the first-grade class with Miss Lippy and he drew a blue duck.

"I drew the duck blue because I've never seen a blue duck before, and to be honest with you, I wanted to see a blue duck."

There are no wrong answers here. No rationalization. No rules. No censorship.

Whatever you envision will be "Quack-tastic! Quack Quack Quack."

Note to self: Add to my personal SWOT strengths quadrant, "Excels at recalling movie quotes."

Anyway, that's the vibe. That's the energy I want you to channel.

You feelin' it? OK, now...

Imagine your life as a blank canvas. What do you want to create? What story do you want to tell? What color do you want your duck to be? This chapter is all about tapping into your imagination, connecting with your deepest desires, and envisioning your ideal life.

Having a clear vision for your ideal life will help you focus on designing a strategic plan and setting goals that work toward bringing your vision to life. Understanding what the ideal outcome is will serve as a roadmap that guides you toward your goals and helps you establish criteria that will help you make decisions that take you closer to your ideal life.

That way, you'll be better equipped to steer clear of things that could take you off track. We'll take a closer look at how to overcome some of those detractors and threats (like our own mind!) in Step 4: Reframe, Reprogram, Rewire.

The Power of Visualization

In marketing, before a campaign is launched or a single ad is created, the team spends time visualizing the end result.

I loved how one of my C-suite mentors would position this part of the process before any huge launch. Sitting at the head seat of the boardroom table, she would ask in her confident, probing, HBIC (aka Head Bitch in Charge) tone, "What's the headline?"

Translation: After we launch this campaign, what are the positive headlines we'd love to see show up in national tier one media outlets? What media coverage are we aiming for?

This was her way of asking, "What's the vision? What's the best possible outcome? What type of impact do we want to make?"

Visualization works the same way in your life. When you take time to picture your ideal future, you're not just wishing. You're priming your mind to notice opportunities, make better decisions, and take inspired action.

Neuroscience shows that our brains often can't distinguish between a vividly imagined experience and a real one. That means the more clearly you can see your ideal life, the more likely you are to create it. This is another thing we'll dive deeper into in Step 4: Reframe, Reprogram, Rewire.

Try this:
Find a quiet spot, close your eyes (again, after you read this), and take a few deep breaths. Picture yourself living your ideal life. Where are you? Who are you with? What are you doing? How do you feel? Let the details fill in naturally, without judgment or limits.

Prompts and Exercises

Now, let's get those creative juices flowing. Use the following prompts to spark your imagination and help you get specific about your vision:

- If I could do anything, be anything, or have anything, what would it be?

- What does a perfect day in my ideal life look like from morning to night?

- What are three things I've always wanted to try but haven't yet?

- Who inspires me, and what about their life do I admire?

- What would I do if I knew I couldn't fail?

Write your answers in a journal, on your phone, or even on sticky notes. The goal is to let your mind wander and see what comes up.

The "If I Could ..." Free Writing Exercise

Set a timer for ten minutes. At the top of your page, write **"If I could ..."**

Now, let your pen move without stopping. Don't edit, don't judge, don't worry about spelling or grammar. Just write whatever comes to mind, even if it seems silly or impossible. The only rule is to keep writing until the timer goes off.

When you're done, read over what you wrote. Notice any patterns, surprises, or ideas that make your heart beat a little faster.

The "If I Weren't Afraid, I Would ..." Exercise

Fear is a sneaky thing. It can keep us from even admitting what we want. Let's call it out.

Write this prompt at the top of a new page: **"If I weren't afraid, I would..."**

Again, set a timer for ten minutes and write without stopping. Be honest with yourself. Sometimes, the things we're most afraid to admit are the things we most need to pursue.

Afterward, reflect on what you wrote. What would it feel like to take even a tiny step toward one of those things?

We're going to talk a lot more about mindset strategies we can use to defeat that bastard named Fear in Step 4: Reframe, Reprogram, Rewire.

Vision Boards: Bringing Your Vision to Life

In marketing, once the big ideas are flowing, teams often create "mood boards." Mood boards are like a vibe check. They're a collage or a collection of visual representations (images, videos, screenshots, etc.) that are aggregated and used for inspiration to help guide the look, feel, and energy a new brand or campaign wants to model.

Instead of copying others, pay attention to what genuinely excites you. Notice the style, tone, and positioning that spark your creativity. Use those elements as inspiration to shape your own unique approach, one that feels authentic to you and attracts the audience and outcomes you truly want.

The adage "a picture is worth a thousand words" is the perfect proof point. Seeing something versus reading something just hits different. So, mood boards help to get everyone aligned to see the vision and sparks excitement and creativity on bringing your brand's own unique version to life.

For instance, one of my clients was a global food manufacturing company and made food products that some of the world's most well-known brands would white label (slap their brand's logo on it as if it was made by them). Before any photo or video shoot, we would create a mood board in the form of a slide deck with the look and feel and brand attributes and styles we wanted the hired photographer or videographer to capture during the shoot. This helped them see our vision and helped them to strategize on the best location, props, lighting, and talent that would align best with the brand vision.

So, think of a vision board as your personal mood board.

The vision board you create is a collection of images, words, and symbols that represent your dreams and goals. Vision boards are powerful because they keep your desires front and center, reminding you daily of what you're working toward.

My Vision Board:
I created mine using Google Slides. I started with a single blank slide, and I searched for photos online that symbolized my dreams and goals. I have pictures of a healthy body, a log cabin with a large front porch and two rocking chairs surrounded by pine trees, a woman skiing, a lake surrounded by mountains, a large library, a picture of beautiful healthy foods, my dream house, a huge stage with a large crowd in the background, a sticker that says *"New York Times* Bestseller." (I need your help with this one. Tell your friends to buy this book. Seriously, help me help you—create an Amazon affiliate link for my book, share it with a friend, and make a few bucks—said in my best Long Island car salesman voice.) You get the idea.

Many people believe that seeing your goals visually helps you manifest them into reality—a concept known as manifestation, another thing we'll talk about in Step 4: Reframe, Reprogram, Rewire. Whether you believe in the magic or just the motivation, there's no denying the power of a clear, visual reminder.

Vision Board Exercise

Old School:
Grab a stack of magazines, scissors, glue, and a poster board. Flip through the magazines and cut out any images, words, or colors that resonate with your vision. Don't overthink it—let your intuition guide you. Arrange and glue them onto your board in a way that feels inspiring. Hang your vision board somewhere you'll see it every day.

New School:
If you prefer digital like me, use a tool like Canva, Pinterest, a photo collage app, or create a slide in PowerPoint or Google Slides. Search for images online that represent your goals and dreams. Arrange them

into a digital collage and set it as your phone or computer wallpaper, or print it out and keep it nearby.

Your vision board isn't about perfection. It's about inspiration. It's a living, breathing reminder of the life you're creating—one bold blue duck at a time.

CALL TO ACTION

IF YOU HAVE THE REBRAND YOU COMPANION WORKBOOK, HEAD TO THE SECTION OF THE CORRESPONDING CHAPTER AND COMPLETE THE ASSOCIATED QUESTIONS AND PROMPTS.

Now it's your turn. Go back to each of these exercises and take the time to complete each one.

Save your work as a separate file in your Rebrand You folder.

In the next chapter, we'll learn how to overcome the fear of change. We'll explore strategies for embracing uncertainty, taking risks, and stepping outside your comfort zone.

CHAPTER 7

Exploring New Possibilities

In this chapter, I'll show you how to think like a marketer to brainstorm new possibilities for your life. We'll look at ways to generate fresh ideas for your direction, using the same creative formulas marketers rely on to develop and pitch brand and campaign concepts. You'll discover how to apply these strategies to design a vision for your own life that excites and inspires you.

This is the part where it becomes really important to revisit the intention you set in Chapter 1 to help solve the challenge and objective you stated. Remember, I said it was going to be the compass that helps us navigate the next steps in the framework? This is like step one of the campaign brief process—what do we want to do and why do we need to do it?

When marketers brainstorm new campaign ideas for a client, they don't start from scratch. They gather all the data they've collected during the market research phase, analyze it to spot patterns, and connect the dots to make educated guesses about what might work. Based on this analysis, they develop creative campaign concepts that align with the client's brand values, mission, market position, audience, and goals.

Typically, a marketing agency or in-house marketer will present three options to the client (or executive team) to choose from. Each idea is supported by a set of assumptions and a rationale that explains why it's a good fit. The team then evaluates the options using a set of criteria, such as alignment with the brand's mission, vision, and values, to determine which idea is most likely to achieve the desired results.

This process uses data, insights, and design thinking to generate ideas that are both innovative and aligned with the client's goals.

In the same way, when you're brainstorming new possibilities for your life, you're not starting from scratch. You're building on everything you've learned about yourself so far, your strengths, weaknesses, values, passions, the patterns you've uncovered, and how you envision your ideal life. You're using this information to make educated guesses about what might work for you.

Revisit Your Challenge and Objective—Dream Big

My assumption is that the majority of people reading this book are likely in the same camp I was. You're interested in using the REBRAND Framework through a career lens, i.e., gaining clarity on the career that best aligns with your purpose and the ideal lifestyle you envision for yourself. Regardless, it's time to revisit the challenge and objective you created for yourself earlier in the book.

Your Challenge and Objective:

Challenge: _____

Objective: _____

OK, now that you've revisited your original challenge and objective, think about the "blue duck" and the "headline" you created for yourself in the last chapter.

What's the best possible outcome you can imagine? Got that vision locked in?

Perfect. Let's move right along, then, shall we?

Review Your Personal SWOT

Before you jump into the brainstorming and ideation process, I want you to look at your SWOT analysis. Then, you're going to use the following guidelines to help you brainstorm new ideas, options, and strategies for your career and life redesign.

- **Focus on Your Strengths:** You will want to spend most of your time and energy on activities that align with your strengths. This will help you feel more energized, confident, and fulfilled.

- **Capitalize on Opportunities:** Look for ways to align your strengths with emerging opportunities. This could mean exploring a new career path, starting a side hustle, or learning a new skill. If you're not sure where to start, don't worry. I'll walk you through some brainstorming exercises in the next section to help spark ideas. And if you ever feel stuck or want more personalized support, you will find details on how to connect with me in the Resources section at the end of this book. You don't have to figure it all out alone!

- **Address Your Weaknesses:** Don't spend too much of your workday on tasks you struggle with. Whenever possible, ask for help or delegate these responsibilities to others. If you want to improve in certain areas, create a simple development plan, but focus on just one or two weaknesses at a time so you don't get overwhelmed.

- **Prepare for Threats:** Identify potential challenges and create contingency plans to address them. This will help you feel more confident and prepared as you move forward.

The Ideation Process

Before we start brainstorming new directions for your life, let's make sure you've gathered a full picture of who you are and what matters to you. Along with your SWOT analysis, tools like ikigai, dharma, and SHAPE (explained in the section below) can help you dig deeper into your purpose, passions, and unique strengths.

Once you've collected all this insight, you'll put on your marketer's hat (personally, mine is a mid-2000s trucker hat. I'd love to know what style your metaphorical marketer hat is!). Next, you're going to use marketing techniques to evaluate and improve your life; don't worry, I'll guide you through it. Just like marketers brainstorm and pitch campaign concepts to clients, you'll create a few "campaign pitches" for your own life, different possible directions or strategies you could pursue.

Let's break down what's involved in a marketing campaign pitch.

Typically, when presenting a brand or campaign idea, marketers or their agency partners will present a few potential campaign concepts.

You can present as many as you want, but too many options become overwhelming, so aim for three concept ideas based on the data and insights from your analysis.

For this example, let's assume you're the brand strategist of an ad agency. You're working with a tech client whose challenge is lagging product adoption in the Midwest region of the United States. The client's objective is to increase brand awareness and product usage in the Midwest market.

Knowing the client's challenge and objective, your job is to present three viable marketing campaign concepts that align with their objective and solve their problem.

During your presentation, the ideal outcome is walking away with a clear choice on the winning concept among the three, but it's rarely that cut-and-dried (kinda like life, right?).

But in a perfect world, these would be the simplified steps for presenting and then selecting a final brand campaign concept:

- **Walk the client through each concept**, explaining how the creative direction could help them overcome their challenge and increase brand awareness and product usage in the Midwest market.

- **Solicit client feedback** on their likes and dislikes, pros and cons of each concept, which can be a combination of objective and subjective inputs and rationale. *(This is also the part where you bite your tongue when they talk about how what their sister's baby's niece's cousin said went viral on TikTok, so we absolutely should do something like that. I know my marketing readers felt that one, deep.)*

- **Narrow down** your potential concepts and eliminate one of the three.

- **Review the two** finalists.

- **Select one concept** to build your entire brand or campaign strategy from across your paid, owned, shared, and earned marketing channels.

If you're lucky to have a client select one with no requested changes or modifications, pat yourself on the back. That's utopia.

What *typically* happens in this process is a Frankenstein approach: They'll like some elements of concept 1, some of concept 2, some of concept 3, and then you create a new concept that marries some of those attributes, and that's what you end up going to market with and launching.

So, that's what we're going to do for you, my friend.

We're going to use the exercises below to create a few different concepts, and then you're going to narrow it down to the one that has the best shot at achieving YOUR objective and personal definition of success. I've found these techniques to be extremely helpful as the starting point for ideating on my own personal rebrand, but feel free to explore other strategies and techniques.

Finding Your Purpose: Ikigai, Dharma and SHAPE

In my quest for finding my purpose, I've watched a ton of podcasts on personal development, spirituality, self-discovery, and more from a number of faiths, practices, teachers, and guides. As I mentioned earlier in this book, have an open mind about the assessment protocol because guess what? While different, they're all essentially pointing us to the same discovery, with slight nuances. So, if we can collectively look at things, it helps bring a more holistic, inclusive approach to the process.

Ikigai and Dharma

I can't remember whose podcast I heard it first, so apologies to Tom Bilyeu or Jay Shetty for not providing the proper attribution. (I don't remember which was first touch or last touch—that's a little joke for the marketing readers—IYKYK.)

But when I first learned about ikigai and dharma after listening to one of their podcasts, it resonated so deeply during a time when I was trying to find what my purpose is and what my next steps could be.

Ikigai

In Japanese culture, the concept of **ikigai** refers to your "reason for being." It's the intersection of four key areas:

- What you love
- What you're good at
- What the world needs
- What you can get paid for

When you find your ikigai, you discover a deep sense of purpose and fulfillment, as your daily activities align with your passions, talents, and the needs of the world.

Dharma

Similarly, in Hindu philosophy, the concept of **dharma** refers to your inherent duty and purpose in life. *Dharma* is a Sanskrit word from Hindu philosophy, often translated as "duty," "righteous path," or "life's purpose." It's the idea that each person has a unique role or calling based on their nature, abilities, and circumstances.

- What is my unique role?
- How can I serve the world?
- What is my true nature?

Living your dharma means acting in alignment with your true self and contributing to the greater good, which brings meaning and satisfaction.

SHAPE
I absolutely love that the YouTube algorithm bequeaths me with diverse channels with content aligned around contextually related content topics. Like when, during the COVID craziness, Saddleback Church Pastor Rick Warren, author of *The New York Times* bestselling book *The Purpose Driven Life*, somehow appeared on my screen and I learned about SHAPE.

SHAPE is a Christian framework developed by Pastor Rick Warren to help individuals discover their unique calling. SHAPE is an acronym that stands for:

- **S**piritual Gifts: the special abilities God has given you

- **H**eart: the passions and interests that motivate you

- **A**bilities: your natural talents and learned skills

- **P**ersonality: the unique way you relate to others and the world

- **E**xperiences: the life events that have shaped you

By understanding your SHAPE, you can serve others through your unique God-given design in a way that is authentic and impactful.

The Common Thread

Do you see what all three of these frameworks have in common?

- They're each designed to help you discover your unique purpose by exploring your passions, strengths, and the ways you can serve others.

- They each encourage self-reflection, self-awareness, and a commitment to making a positive impact in the world.

- Whether spiritual, philosophical, or practical, they all point toward a life of meaning and contribution.

Here's my *Rebrand YOU* aggregate version of the three with the core elements and key questions:

Core Elements

- **Passion:** What do you love? What energizes you?

- **Strengths:** What are your natural talents, skills, and gifts?

- **Values:** What matters most to you? What principles guide your life?

- **Service:** How can you use your strengths and passions to meet the needs of others or the world?

- **Experience:** How have your life experiences shaped your perspective and abilities?

- **Sustainability:** How can you create a life that is both meaningful and sustainable (personally, professionally, and financially)?

Key Questions

- What activities make me lose track of time?

- What do people often ask me for help with?

- What problems in the world am I drawn to solve?

- How can I use my unique combination of gifts, passions, and experiences to serve others?

- What would a rebranded, purpose-driven version of my life look like?

My Personal Answers to These Questions

Take a moment to consider your own answers to these key questions as you read mine. Notice what stands out for you, and jot down any ideas or patterns that come up.

Key Questions and My Personal Answers

What activities make me lose track of time?
Writing, speaking, coaching, deep conversations, learning, creating content, helping others, and making people laugh.

What do people often ask me for help with?
Marketing, communications, career advice, community building, leadership development, and personal growth.

What problems in the world am I drawn to solve?
Helping people live authentic, successful, and peaceful lives without burnout and suffering; connecting people to their full potential; improving communication; reframing limiting beliefs; and promoting well-being.

How can I use my unique gifts, passions, and experiences to serve others?
By sharing my story, mentoring, creating educational content and experiences, speaking, and using humor to make growth accessible for people and organizations.

What would a rebranded, purpose-driven version of my life look like?
I am a thought leader and mentor, running a thriving business that empowers others. I am financially independent, aligned with my values, making a positive impact, and balancing work with well-being.

Core Elements and My Personal Answers

Passion: What do I love? What energizes me?
I'm deeply passionate about self-development, business, spirituality, kindness, growth, and comedy. I love learning, truth-seeking, creating content, and helping others grow. Writing, speaking, teaching, and sharing my healing journey and new things I'm learning to support people and organizations energize me. I'm obsessed with "life design optimization" and the practical application of psychology and spirituality for well-being.

Strengths: What are my natural talents, skills, and gifts?
I excel at speaking, motivating, writing, coaching, training, and simplifying complex ideas. I'm a good listener, curious, and make others feel included. My expertise lies in marketing, communications, connecting people, and community building. I also use humor to make work and personal growth fun and approachable.

Values: What matters most to me? What principles guide my life?
I value justice, truth, freedom, peace, love, fairness, and positive thinking. Personal and spiritual growth, authenticity, resilience, and adapt-

ability are key. I believe in the power of mindset, reframing limiting beliefs, and the importance of gratitude and high-vibe energy.

Service: How can I use my strengths and passions to meet the needs of others or the world?
I can leverage my marketing and communication expertise to help people and businesses grow. I aim to educate, entertain, and empower professionals by sharing my experiences and practical blueprints for success and well-being. I can help people design lives and careers aligned with their values, free from burnout, through frameworks, mentorship, writing, and speaking. I can help companies transform culture and brands through authentic leadership, emotional intelligence, and practical communication strategies. And I can use humor to make growth and transformation fun!

Experience: How have my life experiences shaped my perspective and abilities?
Overcoming childhood struggles, job loss, and health challenges has made me resilient, empathetic, and confident. My journey from corporate success to entrepreneurship, coupled with my physical, mental, and spiritual healing, has taught me to trust myself and embrace change. I now see myself as a "rising phoenix," ready to help others transform.

Sustainability: How can I create a life that is both meaningful and sustainable (personally, professionally, and financially)?
I envision a "knowledge business" where I earn a living through writing, speaking, consulting, comedy, and coaching. I'll balance my career with well-being, healthy habits, and spiritual growth, using tools like vision boards, journaling, and goal tracking to stay focused on abundance.

CORE ELEMENT	EXAMPLE
Passion	Self-development, growth, comedy, spirituality, helping others, neuroscience, learning, writing, speaking
Strengths	Motivating, writing, coaching, marketing, community building, humor, empathy
Values	Justice, truth, freedom, peace, love, authenticity, growth, gratitude
Service	Educating, empowering, mentoring, creating frameworks, using humor to teach and connect
Experience	Overcoming adversity, corporate success, entrepreneurship, healing journey, resilience
Sustainability	Knowledge business, speaking, writing, coaching, healthy habits, vision boards, journaling, goal tracking

Pulling It All Together to Come Up with Your Three Concepts

Now that you have a framework for thinking about your purpose, it's time to brainstorm new possibilities or, as I used in the marketing campaign presentation example, your three concepts to present to the client (aka you).

As you brainstorm, use your responses to the core elements and key questions you just read about, and then keep these questions at the forefront of your mind:

- What's on your heart?

- What is your big dream?

- What problem do you want to solve?

- What are you passionate about?

Here are some techniques to help you generate ideas:

- **Mind Mapping:** Start with a central idea or question and branch out with related ideas, concepts, and associations.

- **Freewriting:** Set a timer for ten to fifteen minutes and write continuously without editing or censoring yourself.

- **Reverse Brainstorming:** Instead of brainstorming solutions to a problem, brainstorm all the ways you could make the problem worse. This can help you identify potential pitfalls and generate creative solutions.

* **AI Tools like ChatGPT:** Prompt an AI tool with questions that ask what job opportunities exist for *[insert your responses to core elements and key questions, SWOT, assessment data, and any other inputs related to your challenge and objective.]*

My Type A Ass's Recommendation: Leverage the work you've already done and use AI. The amount of insight and data you receive in seconds versus hours or days is freaking mind-blowing—and so damn helpful for me and my clients!

Here's an example of how I used an AI prompt to help me come up with my career concepts and narrow down my choices to help me figure out what to do next with my career:

ChatGPT Prompt:
You're an expert career adviser and strategist who helps connect people to their ideal job based on factors like their unique purpose, passions, strengths, service to others, and ideal lifestyle.

Based on their objective and challenge [insert objective and challenge] and the following data inputs [insert all of the assessment data results, SWOT, etc.] do the following:

Provide five different career options for this person that best align with their purpose, values, zone of genius, lifestyle goals, and how much money they could make.

Provide suggestions for the types of jobs, industries, companies, macro- and micro-factors about industry growth or contraction, and any additional factors you would recommend based on your expertise as a career adviser and strategist.

Prioritize opportunities in growing industries and skillsets by looking at macro-environmental factors and demand in specific skills or industries.

Provide your five different career options in a table format and rank them in the order of priority of which you think best aligns with financial opportunity and career satisfaction and stability.

Note: I added the fifth one for shits and giggles.

Here were my results from ChatGPT:

Career & Path Description	Potential Income Range	Industries & Companies	Macro/Micro Factors	Why This Fits You
Thought Leadership & Knowledge Business *(Coach, Speaker, Author, Online Course Creator, Podcast Host)* Build a personal brand around life design, neuroscience, and personal growth. Monetize through coaching, speaking, digital products, workshops, and content creation (books, podcasts, courses).	$100-$500K+ (scalable; top earners $1M+) Income grows with audience, product suite, and partnerships.	Personal development, EdTech, wellness, creator economy. Companies: Mindvalley, MasterClass, LinkedIn Learning, or your own brand.	Macro: Explosive growth in online education, coaching, and creator economy. AI tools make scaling easier. Demand for authentic, relatable thought leaders is rising. Micro: Your story, humor, and expertise are highly marketable.	Leverages your strengths in communication, teaching, and storytelling. High autonomy, creative freedom, and impact. Aligns with your desire to inspire, educate, and empower at scale. Flexible, abundant, and purpose-driven.

Career & Path Description	Potential Income Range	Industries & Companies	Macro/Micro Factors	Why This Fits You
Chief Marketing Officer (CMO) (Corporate Leadership in Marketing Strategy, Brand Management, Digital Marketing) Lead marketing initiatives, drive revenue growth, and build brand awareness for a company.	$150K-$500K+ (corporate/tech/start-up; equity possible) Top-tier CMOs at large corporations can earn significantly more (>$1M) with bonuses and equity.	Tech, consumer goods, healthcare, finance SaaS, and any company that requires a strong marketing presence.	Macro: Marketing is constantly evolving with new technologies and platforms (AI, social media, data analytics). Demand for skilled CMOs remains high, especially those with digital expertise. Micro: Your ability to adapt to new marketing trends, leverage data-driven insights, and build high-performing teams will be critical.	Directly utilizes your 20+ years of marketing experience. High earning potential, especially in larger companies. Aligns with your ENFJ personality and desire to inspire others. You can significantly impact a company's growth and brand reputation.
Chief Community/ Wellness Officer or Head of People & Culture (Corporate or Start-up Leadership in Employee Experience or Well-being) Lead culture, learning, and well-being initiatives in a mission-driven company. Design programs that foster growth, resilience, and positive energy.	$120K-$300K+ (corporate/tech/start-up; equity possible) Consulting:$150-$500/hr	Tech, health and wellness, future of work, HR tech, conscious business. Companies: Calm, Headspace, Notion, Asana, B-corp start-ups, or consult for multiple firms.	Macro: Companies are investing in employee well-being and culture to attract/retain talent. The "future of work" is people-centric. Micro: Your empathy, leadership, and communication skills are in high demand.	Uses your people skills, vision, and passion for well-being. High impact on organizational culture and individual lives. Stable income, benefits, and potential for consulting/freelance flexibility.

Career & Path Description	Potential Income Range	Industries & Companies	Macro/Micro Factors	Why This Fits You
Edutainment Content Creator & Brand Collaborator (YouTube, TikTok, Podcast, Comedy-Infused Education, Brand Partnerships) Create engaging, humorous, and educational content on neuroscience, life design, and personal growth. Monetize via ads, sponsorships, live events, and digital products.	$60K–$300K+ (varies by audience size, sponsorships, product sales) Top creators earn $500K+	Creator economy, media, wellness, EdTech, entertainment. Companies: YouTube, Spotify, Patreon, brands in wellness/education.	Macro: Short-form video, podcasting, and "edutainment" are booming. Brands seek authentic creators for partnerships. Micro: Your entertainer/teacher blend is rare and in demand.	Combines your love of humor, teaching, and content creation. Scalable, creative, and high impact. Flexible lifestyle, potential for rapid growth with the right niche and consistency.

Rebrand You

Career & Path Description	Potential Income Range	Industries & Companies	Macro/Micro Factors	Why This Fits You
Zen-Seeker, Parental Couch Dweller & Pierogi Artist (Rent out your house, move back to Pittsburgh and live with your Dad-Dad, and sling pierogies with a smile.) Embrace a simpler, less expensive life, and live off the rental income from your house in Arizona. Focus on mastering the art of pierogi making and perfecting your Pittsburghese language.	$25K–$40K (plus pierogi perks!) Income dependent on pierogi sales and tips.	Food service, Pittsburgh tourism, comfort food. Companies: S&D Polish Deli, Pierogies Plus, or start your own pierogi empire.	Macro: Pittsburgh is experiencing a cultural renaissance, with a growing appreciation for its culinary heritage. Pierogies are always in demand. Micro: Your ability to connect with people and make them laugh could translate into excellent customer service and pierogi sales.	Why This Fits (Humorously): Immediate Stress Relief: No more strategic planning, just delicious dumplings. Pittsburgh Roots: A return to your roots could provide a sense of comfort and nostalgia. Low-Pressure Environment: Focus on simple tasks and direct customer interaction. Pierogi Perks: Unlimited access to warm, buttery pierogies (a definite plus!). "Target Is Peaceful" Vibes: Sometimes the idea of a simple, predictable job is appealing when facing career uncertainty.

Not too bad, right? Based on my passions, values, strengths, current market conditions, and the other inputs, these are all viable options or "concepts" to consider.

The next step is to eliminate two, so we narrow down the top three choices to present to the client (aka you).

Create Clear Criteria or a Scorecard to Evaluate Your Options

Once you've brainstormed new possibilities, it's time to evaluate them. It's helpful to have a clear set of criteria and a scorecard to evaluate each option against.

Career Option Evaluation Criteria
Rate Each Option: 1 (Very Low), 2 (Low), 3 (Moderate), 4 (High), or 5 (Very High) for each criterion below.

Alignment with Core Values and Purpose
Does this option allow you to live your values (authenticity, growth, service, well-being, freedom, etc.) and fulfill your sense of purpose?

- **1:** Conflicts with your core values; feels meaningless or misaligned

- **3:** Neutral; some alignment, but compromises required

- **5:** Deeply aligned; feels like a calling and supports your highest values

Lifestyle Fit and Flexibility
Does this option support your ideal lifestyle (work-life balance, autonomy, location, travel, well-being, etc.)?

- **1:** Rigid, high-stress, or incompatible with your desired lifestyle
- **3:** Some flexibility, but notable trade-offs
- **5:** Highly flexible; supports your ideal daily rhythm and well-being

Financial Opportunity
Does this option meet or exceed your income goals and offer financial security or growth?

- **1:** Well below your needs; unstable or capped
- **3:** Meets minimum needs, but limited upside
- **5:** Exceeds goals; scalable, secure, or offers significant upside

Use of Strengths and Zone of Genius
Does this option let you use your best skills, talents, and passions most of the time?

- **1:** Rarely uses your strengths; feels draining or unfulfilling
- **3:** Uses some strengths, but not consistently
- **5:** Fully leverages your unique gifts and energizes you

Positive Impact and Service
Does this option allow you to make a meaningful difference for others or the world?

- **1:** Little or no positive impact; feels disconnected from service
- **3:** Some impact, but not central to the role
- **5:** High, direct positive impact; service is core to the work

Growth and Learning Potential
Will this option challenge you, help you grow, and keep you engaged?

- **1:** Stagnant; little room for growth or learning
- **3:** Some growth, but may plateau
- **5:** High potential for personal and professional development

Industry and Market Outlook
Is this field/role in a growing, stable, or declining industry?

- **1:** Declining or unstable industry
- **3:** Stable, but not growing
- **5:** Rapidly growing, future-proof, or in high demand

How to Use

- **Rate Each Option:** *1 (Very Low), 2 (Low), 3 (Moderate), 4 (High)*, or *5 (Very High)* for each criterion above.

- **Assign Weights:** If some criteria matter more to you than others, like financial opportunity or values alignment, you can give those a higher weight. For example, if financial opportunity is twice as important as lifestyle, you could multiply its score by two. If you are not sure how to do this or want to keep it simple, just use the basic scores without weighting.

- **Add Up the Scores:** Tally the scores (or weighted scores) for each option.

- **Compare Titles:** See which options are the best fit for you based on the highest to lowest score.

Example:

If "Thought Leadership and Knowledge Business" scores five for values, five for lifestyle, four for financial, five for strengths, five for impact, five for growth, and five for industry, its total would be 34/35, which would make it a top contender.

Here's My Official Scorecard:

Criteria	Leadership/ Knowledge	CMO	Community/ Wellness	Edutainment Content Creator	Pittsburgh Pierogi Artist
1. Alignment with Core Values and Purpose	5	4	5	4	2
2. Lifestyle Fit and Flexibility	5	3	4	5	5
3. Financial Opportunity	4	5	4	3	1
4. Use of Strengths and Zone of Genius	5	4	4	5	2
5. Positive Impact and Service	5	4	5	4	3
6. Growth and Learning Potential	5	4	4	5	2
7. Industry and Market Outlook	5	4	4	5	2
Total Score	**34**	**28**	**30**	**31**	**17**

How to Interpret My Scores:

- **Thought Leadership and Knowledge Business: 34/35**—Top fit for my values, lifestyle, strengths, and market opportunity

- **Edutainment Content Creator: 31/35**—High on lifestyle, strengths, and growth, but a bit less on financial security

- **Community/Wellness Officer: 30/35**—Strong on values, impact, and stability, but less flexible and slightly less financial upside

- **Chief Marketing Officer (CMO): 28/35**—High financial opportunity and uses my experience, but less lifestyle flexibility and slightly less alignment with my core purpose

- **Pittsburgh Pierogi Artist: 17/35**—High on lifestyle simplicity, but low on financial, growth, and alignment with my bigger purpose (though it's a great "reset" option!)

How to Use It:

- **Remove the two lowest-scoring options** from your concept brainstorm. You will not be focusing on these as your main direction right now, but that does not mean you have to give them up completely. If one of your ideas is something you truly love, like painting, consider how it might fit into your life as a hobby, a side project, or a future goal. Sometimes, the things that light us up can grow with practice, learning, or even as a reward for reaching other milestones. Remember, your passions can take many forms, and you can always revisit them later.

- **Compare the top three** and reflect on which feels most exciting and sustainable.

- **Choose the one** that best matches your current priorities—or use the numbers as a starting point for deeper reflection.

- **Create a Frankenstein version** and create a new option/concept that is a hybrid of the elements that felt most exciting and sustainable to you. (Remember I mentioned this is often what can happen after presenting the final three concepts to the client? You leave the meeting with more work and have to figure out another concept. It takes a little more work, but it's typically worth it because you're marrying the best elements from each concept and creating a SUPER version that's an even better fit.)

Here's How I Used Mine:
So, I removed the CMO and Pittsburgh Pierogi Artist options. Obviously, the Pittsburgh Pierogi Artist was an easy one to remove, but I had to really reflect on why the CMO role wasn't a viable concept to present.

My fantasy of living at home with my Dad-Dad rent- and bills-free is fun to imagine because it feels like so much pressure and stress would be alleviated from the financial side of "figuring out" how to earn money with a stress-free lifestyle, but I would not be living up to my full potential and making an impact. I'd be helping other people by making them the best damn perogies they've ever had (hello, high-achiever here!), but it's not aligned with my zone of genius, and I could help people in a much more impactful way by tapping into my personal SHAPE, ikigai, and dharma.

And while yes, I'm qualified to take a CMO role at a great company with a high-salary potential, great benefits, and more stability than entrepreneurship (scratch that word *stability* and replace it with *predictability* because you can lose your job at any time in corporate as I found out), which sounds enticing, it's not super aligned for me like it once was.

I already achieved the corner office and the CMO title I thought would make me feel worthy. And newsflash: Nope. While the predictability, multimillion-dollar budgets, big teams, awards, and all the frills sound nice on paper, it also means navigating corporate politics again, less lifestyle flexibility, a cap on my earning potential, and less bandwidth to focus on my creative side projects and how I want to dabble in other things that light me up and excite me.

So, with those two options eliminated, I narrowed down these options to present to the client (aka me):

- **Thought Leadership and Knowledge Business: 34/35—** Top fit for my values, lifestyle, strengths, and market opportunity

- **Edutainment Content Creator: 31/35—**High on lifestyle, strengths, and growth, but a bit less on financial security

- **Community/Wellness Officer: 30/35—**Strong on values, impact, and stability, but less flexible and slightly less financial upside

Presenting Three Concepts to the Client (You)— and Selecting the Winner to Activate

I'll get right to the punchline: I created a Frankenstein concept just as I suspected I would. There were elements that I liked from each option. So, I took the elements I liked and patched them together for the concept to build a go-to-market strategy around.

I asked ChatGPT to help me create a hybrid role or career that includes all of the elements of my top three concepts, plus adds comedy into the mix.

I asked it to fuse all of my favorite elements of the concepts— thought leadership, CMO-level marketing, community/wellness leadership, edutainment, and comedy—into a single, high-impact, high-earning, and totally unique role.

The results are incredible.

Chief Edutainment Officer and Stand-Up Storyteller

Other Title Ideas:

- Chief Edutainment Officer

- Stand-Up Storyteller-in-Chief

- Head of Growth, Laughter, and Learning

- Chief Well-Being and Comedy Officer

- Founder and CEO, Edutainment Group

Role Overview
You are the face and architect of a next-generation personal development brand that blends neuroscience, life design, and well-being with world-class marketing, community leadership, and comedy. You operate as a public thought leader, C-suite marketing strategist, community builder, and comedic edutainer—onstage, online, and in the boardroom.

Key Responsibilities

- **Thought Leadership and Content Creation:**
  Develop and deliver signature talks, workshops, online courses, and books that blend science-backed personal growth with humor and storytelling. Host a top-rated

podcast and YouTube channel where you interview experts, riff on neuroscience, and make self-development fun and accessible.

- **CMO-Level Brand Strategy:**
Lead all marketing, brand partnerships, and digital strategy for your own brand (or a mission-driven company). Oversee campaigns, product launches, and audience growth using cutting-edge AI, data analytics, and creative storytelling.

- **Community and Culture Leadership:**
Design and nurture a global community focused on well-being, resilience, and positive energy. Lead retreats, masterminds, and online forums that foster deep connection and growth.

- **Edutainment and Stand-up Comedy:**
Perform stand-up routines and comedic keynotes at conferences, festivals, and corporate events. Use humor to break down barriers, challenge limiting beliefs, and make neuroscience and life design approachable for all.

- **Brand Collaborations and Partnerships:**
Collaborate with wellness, tech, and EdTech brands for co-branded content, campaigns, and live events. Serve as a spokesperson and creative consultant for companies seeking to infuse their culture and marketing with humor and humanity.

Income Streams

- High-ticket coaching, consulting, and speaking engagements ($10K–$50K+ per event)

- Digital products, online courses, and membership communities ($100K–$500K+ per year)

- Brand partnerships, sponsorships, and affiliate marketing ($5K–$100K+ per year, depending on audience size and engagement)

- Book deals, podcast ad revenue, and live event ticket sales ($1K–$250K+ per year, depending on reach, sales, and event scale)

- Equity or retainer as a fractional CMO or chief community officer for select companies ($2K–$20K per month, per client, or equity states that on average can range from 0.5 percent to 5 percent+, depending on company size and agreement)

Industries and Companies

- Personal development, EdTech, wellness, creator economy, media, tech, and entertainment

- Companies: Mindvalley, MasterClass, Calm, Headspace, Notion, LinkedIn Learning, YouTube, Spotify, or your own brand

Macro/Micro Factors

- **Macro:** Surging demand for authentic, relatable thought leaders and edutainers. Online education, wellness, and the creator economy are booming. Companies are investing in well-being, culture, and innovative marketing.

- **Micro:** Your unique blend of expertise, humor, and leadership is rare and highly marketable. You can scale your impact and income while staying true to your values and passions.

Why This Role Is a Perfect Fit

- **Leverages All Your Strengths:** Communication, teaching, marketing, leadership, humor, and creativity

- **High Autonomy and Flexibility:** Design your own schedule, projects, and collaborations

- **Massive Impact:** Inspire, educate, and entertain at scale, while building a legacy brand

- **Financial Abundance:** Multiple scalable income streams, with potential for $500K+ annually

- **Fun and Fulfillment:** Everyday blends purpose, play, and positive impact

I mean, come on! Is this not the absolute dream job…for me? If you're a corporate decision-maker reading this book, please create this job description at your company immediately! I would 100% consider going back to corporate if this job description existed. But to my knowledge, it doesn't exist. So, I'll create it myself through my own brand. This is the power of going through these exercises. It doesn't get more specific and perfect than this … for me!

It's now time to figure out the perfect dream job for…you. Because YOU are the main character in this story, my friend!

CALL TO ACTION

IF YOU HAVE **THE REBRAND YOU COMPANION WORKBOOK,** HEAD TO THE SECTION OF THE CORRESPONDING CHAPTER AND COMPLETE THE ASSOCIATED QUESTIONS AND PROMPTS.

It's your turn. You're going to walk through the same process I did, so you can brainstorm concepts, narrow them down to a few, and then select one to create a strategy around and activate in Step 5: Activate Your Aligned Strategy.

What to Do Now:

- Open up your Rebrand You folder.

- Start from the beginning exercise of this chapter.

- And save the final concept selection in your folder, which we'll work on in Step 5: Activate Your Aligned Strategy.

I know you'll feel as excited as I did to see your perfect job description laid out before your eyes. It feels amazing, which is why we'll need to identify any weaknesses or threats that could stand in the way of us signing the offer letter or creating the company where we can LIVE our dream job. As I mentioned before, oftentimes, *we* are our own threat and weakness—or rather, *our mind* and old programming is.

That's why we're going to address that in the next section before we jump into our activation strategy. So, take your time, complete the steps, and save your work in your Rebrand You folder.

We're starting a new section in the REBRAND Framework, Step 4: Reframe, Reprogram, Rewire, next. In Chapter 8: Why Mindset Is Essential to Success, we're going to identify the limiting beliefs and fears that could be holding you back, and we're going to talk about how to reframe, reprogram, and rewire your mind to align with your dream job and redesigned life!

STEP 4

R
E
B
Reframe, Reprogram, Rewire
A
N
D

CHAPTER 8

Why Mindset Is Essential to Success

Welcome to Step 4: Reframe, Reprogram, Rewire!

I'm so glad you're still with me because this may be my favorite section of the book. Why? Because it's all about our mind! Neuroscience, baby! Understanding the power of our thoughts and how to repattern the unhelpful ones, so that we can be primed for the best chance of success of our new rebrand concept becoming a reality when we get to the Activate Your Aligned Strategy section.

Let me give you a serious example of how much I know mindset matters in whether or not we accomplish our goals or live the life we want. It matters to me so much that I invested hundreds of hours studying and thousands of dollars to get certified as a Master Practitioner of Neuro-Linguistic Programming (NLP), Mental Emotional Release®, and Hypnotherapy by the Association for Integrative Psychology.

And you know the coolest thing ever? It was by going through this REBRAND Framework that I was able to connect the dots between my love for neuroscience and self-development with the modality of NLP. The exercises you just read about led me to realize those certifications were a possibility for me and a bridge for the work that's always been on my heart that I wanted to do. I'll share more about the steps that led me down this path in Step 5: Activate Your Aligned Strategy.

The chapters in this section each cover the three pillars of mindset success: reframing, reprogramming, and rewiring. These terms are often used interchangeably in the world of mindset and personal growth, but they each play a unique role in the process of changing your life.

If we filter this through the lens of launching a new brand or marketing campaign for your life, think of them like this:

- **Reframing** is the creative brainstorming: seeing your challenges in a new light.

- **Reprogramming** is the strategy session: deciding what messages you want to send out to the world (and yourself).

- **Rewiring** is the campaign execution: repeating those messages and actions until they become your new normal.

Another quick way to differentiate each of them: Reframing changes your *perspective*, reprogramming changes your *beliefs*, and rewiring changes your *brain*.

All three are essential steps in the REBRAND Framework for creating real, lasting transformation, inside and out.

Mindset Can Make or Break You

Muriel Maignan Wilkins argues in *Leadership Unblocked: Break Through the Beliefs That Limit Your Potential* that limiting beliefs and negative mindsets are among the top obstacles preventing professionals from advancing in their careers. Such beliefs can lead to self-sabotage, erode confidence, and contribute to poor decision-making, ultimately keeping individuals from reaching their full potential[10].

Ouch.

I bet you're beginning this section totally psyched about the "final concept" you landed on for your rebrand, and while you're excited, you can't help but feel doubt about the possibility of a rebranded, re-designed life.

You're silently telling yourself not to get your hopes up. You're already writing in your journal about how the timing isn't right, you don't have X, still need to do Y, or it would be easier to just stay where you're at for the "future" benefits you'll receive when you're in your mid- to late sixties.

Depending on how old you are now, that could be a long freaking time!

And, sadly, if you've neglected yourself for so long and let the stress compound, you likely won't even have the physical health or stamina to enjoy the decades-long sacrifices and fruits of your labor. Even sadder, some of us will work ourselves so hard at the wrong thing, our bodies don't even make it to the "retirement" finish line; our bodies will permanently retire from this planet.

I know it sounds morbid, my friend. But it's the truth. And I've heard way too many stories of this unfolding to the point it breaks my damn heart.

---

10 Muriel M. Wilkins, *Leadership Unblocked: Break Through the Beliefs That Limit Your Potential* (Boston: Harvard Business Review Press, 2025).

But it doesn't have to be that way.

By taking control of your mind, you can take control of your stress. And by taking control of your stress, you're taking control of your health.

Just like marketers need to refine their messaging and positioning as part of a rebrand or new campaign launch, you can refresh and shift your mindset and beliefs in the same way. Think of your mind as your internal brand playbook.

If you are still running on old messaging, outdated programming, limiting beliefs, or unhealed stories, it is no wonder you feel stuck or doubtful about your new direction. That old playbook is probably collecting dust and holding you back from the life that you truly want.

It's time to retire those tired scripts and upgrade your internal messaging. Let go of the beliefs that no longer serve you, and start telling yourself a new story that is aligned with where you are going next. This is your chance to reposition who the hell you are. It's time to transform and rebrand into your higher self.

CALL TO ACTION

IF YOU HAVE **THE REBRAND YOU COMPANION WORKBOOK,** HEAD TO THE SECTION OF THE CORRESPONDING CHAPTER AND COMPLETE THE ASSOCIATED QUESTIONS AND PROMPTS.

Hey, guess what? You can breathe a sigh of relief. There's technically no homework for you to do!

All I want you to do is take four long, deep breaths—inhale for four seconds and exhale for four seconds. And I want you to keep that beautiful open-mindedness you've embodied up to this point.
In the next chapter, you're going to learn how to reframe the way you see things and how much such a simple shift in perspective can improve your life.

CHAPTER 9

Reframe—Change the Lens

I'm sure I don't have to explain this to you because you can likely point to more than a few examples from your own life experience. But damn. Life throws curveballs. That's the euphemistic way to say: Life can totally blindside you with a right hook to the face that makes you see stars, knocks you on your ass, and when you come to and get back on your feet, you're like "Man, I didn't see that one coming!"

I bet you can think of a time or two when a relationship, job, or your health felt like it was on the right track and going well. You're feeling really good and like "Ah, finally some of that *good good!*"

And then, BAM! An unexpected event that feels like a TKO from Mike Tyson (the pre-Jake-Paul-Netflix-fight Tyson).

"Didn't see that coming. What the actual fuck?"

And then, that same old story starts replaying in your head. *Why can't I ever have peace? Why does this keep happening to me? I'm not where I should be. How could this happen to ME?*

Sound familiar?

Yes, something bad just happened that you didn't expect, but I also bet you can think of a few times in your life that the thing you were so distraught about happening when you were going through it ended up being the biggest blessing in disguise after you got through the suck after time passed.

So, the story you tell yourself about your life is just that—a story. And you have the power to change the narrative and your perspective about the things that happen in your life. And that's where reframing comes in.

What Reframing Really Is

Reframing involves facing reality honestly and allowing yourself to feel and process difficult emotions. This practice encourages you to acknowledge what is challenging, reflect on your experience, and then explore what the situation might be teaching you or what new opportunities could come from it. Growth happens when you give yourself space to feel, learn, and gradually shift your perspective.

Reframing is about seeing a negative situation through a lens like "This freaking sucks. This doesn't seem fair. I hate how this is making me feel." Feel the ick and process the emotions—you need to clear that shit out. (More on that when we talk about the impact of unprocessed trauma and emotions and the implications it has on a cellular level in terms of causing disease.) As you navigate the heaviness, notice what it might be bringing to light that you otherwise might have missed.

Reframing isn't about viewing the world through rose-colored glasses. You may have heard the terms toxic positivity or spiritual bypassing, which essentially refer to having an overly optimistic or delulu view of a negative situation or event.

Brands do this all the time. For instance, when a product launch flops, smart marketers don't just give up. They reevaluate their go-to-market strategy and product-market fit. Then they can either reposition it, find a new audience, or highlight a different benefit. They don't just throw in the towel. You can do the same with your life. You can reframe and reposition.

Real-Life Reframing Example

Imagine you're a mid-career professional who just got passed over for a promotion. The default story might be "I'm not good enough. I'll never move up." But what if you reframed it? What if you saw it as a sign that you're meant for something bigger and better, or as a nudge to finally pursue that side hustle you've been dreaming about? Or it helped you realize the way you saw yourself was not aligned with how your organization's leadership saw you.

That experience gave you data. You were able to spot a weakness and work on it. You turned a weakness into an opportunity. Suddenly, the setback becomes a setup for your next big move or to uplevel your hard or soft skills that are needed to take you to the next step in your desired career path.

The Power of Perspective

If you've ever watched a movie twice and noticed something completely different the second time, you already know the power of perspective. The facts didn't change; the way you saw them did. That's reframing in action. It's the art of looking at your life through a new lens, one that highlights your strengths, your growth, and your potential instead of your failures or flaws.

Companies do this all the time. They don't always change the product. They reframe. They change the story around it. They rebrand. You can do the same with your life. Instead of seeing setbacks as proof you're not good enough, you can see them as evidence you're learning, growing, and being redirected to a path more aligned for you right now.

So to recap:

- Reframing is the creative brainstorming: seeing your challenges in a new light.

Reframing changes your *perspective*.

CALL TO ACTION

IF YOU HAVE THE REBRAND YOU COMPANION WORKBOOK, HEAD TO THE SECTION OF THE CORRESPONDING CHAPTER AND COMPLETE THE ASSOCIATED QUESTIONS AND PROMPTS.

Practice reframing your perspective. Find a new way to look at a past or present situation in your life. For instance, instead of "I failed," try "I learned something valuable."

- Grab your journal.

- Write down a recent challenge or disappointment.

- Now, challenge yourself to find at least two alternative ways to view the situation.

- What could you learn from it?

- How might it be working *for* you, not *against* you?

- If your best friend was in your shoes, what would you tell them?

Once you've practiced how to reframe your perspective, I'm going to teach you how to reprogram the unhelpful patterns of thinking you've held onto for years. See you in Chapter 10: Reprogram—Rewrite the Script.

CHAPTER 10

Reprogram—Rewrite the Script

In the last chapter, you learned that reframing is about our perspective and changing the lens. Now you're going to learn that reprogramming is about our beliefs and changing the script. This is where you get honest about the **limiting beliefs** running the show in your mind and recognizing and overcoming **fear**.

Limiting beliefs—destructive thoughts we hold about ourselves that negatively shape our self-perception—can hinder personal growth and professional advancement by reinforcing emotional baggage and self-doubt.[11]

Most of us are walking around with a bunch of outdated, limiting beliefs we picked up from childhood, society, or past failures. These beliefs are like pop-up ads in your brain, constantly telling you what you *can't* do.

Some common limiting beliefs include:

- *I'm not good enough.*

- *I don't have enough time.*

---

11 Melanie A. McNally, "Overcoming Self-Limiting Beliefs," Psychology Today, November 22, 2023, accessed October 4, 2025, https://www.psychologytoday.com/us/blog/empower-your-mind/202311/overcoming-self-limiting-beliefs..

- *I'll fail if I try.*

- *I'm too old (or too young) to do this.*

- *I don't deserve success.*

Reprogramming is the process of identifying those old beliefs and consciously choosing new ones that support your growth and happiness.

As a marketer, I like to think of reprogramming as a brand updating its core messaging. If a company realizes its old tagline or key messaging no longer resonates the way it used to, it creates a new tagline or messaging strategy that better reflects its updated mission, vision, and values.

The Science of Early Programming

Did you know that by the age of seven, most of our subconscious programming is already in place? During those early years, our brains are like sponges, absorbing everything around us. Our experiences, the words we hear, and the emotions we feel imprint upon us.

This means that the beliefs we form as children—about ourselves, others, and the world—can stay with us for the rest of our lives. Unfortunately, it's rare for anyone to have had an absolutely "perfect" childhood. Many of us experienced some form of trauma—some to an unthinkable horrific degree. Some of us can vividly remember traumatic events in our early years. And some of us experienced them, but we completely disassociated and repressed the traumatic events and don't even remember they occurred. But no matter what level of trauma you experienced, if you don't work to uncover and heal it, it can negatively impact you for the rest of your life.

For example, if you grew up in an environment where money was scarce, you might develop a belief that "there's never enough" or "I'll never be financially secure."

Or let's say you experienced rejection or neglect, you might develop a belief that "I'm not lovable" or "I'm not good enough."

Perhaps you always heard one of your parents saying things like "All the hot guys cheat" or "All women are gold diggers." You might develop a belief that "relationships aren't safe," which forces you to put up a wall and block yourself from ever getting close enough to feel true love and intimacy.

These beliefs become the lens through which we see the world. In NLP, we call this a person's internal representation. These beliefs can impact every area of our lives: our careers, our relationships, our health, and our happiness.

Limiting Beliefs Block Happiness and Achieving Our Potential

Have you ever felt like something was holding you back, but you couldn't quite put your finger on it? Perhaps it's the opposite. You know exactly what you want, but you make excuses and create stories about why you can't have the things you want.

Maybe you've set big goals for yourself, but no matter how hard you try, you can't seem to make progress. Or maybe you've achieved success on the outside, but deep down, you still feel unfulfilled.

Chances are the culprit is your limiting beliefs.

Limiting beliefs are the invisible barriers that hold us back from achieving our full potential. They're the negative thoughts and assumptions we have about ourselves, others, and the world around us. They're the stories we tell ourselves that keep us stuck in the same old patterns.

I have lots of friends who are teachers, and I was texting with one recently, and she said:

"I find it very hard to have any time being a working mom to think about what I could even do besides teaching. I also think it's very challenging to leave teaching, which has a good retirement, and I need it to support my family."

Can you spot her limiting beliefs? And this is so NOT judgement because we ALL have limiting beliefs.

Here's what I decoded from her text:

- I don't have time.

- I can't focus on myself because I'm a working mom.

- It's hard to leave my teaching job.

- I need *this* job to support my family.

- I probably won't find another job with good benefits.

- I don't know what I want to do, so it's easier to stick with what I'm already doing.

I guarantee you've said things like that before. I know I have. We all have limiting beliefs. Did you pick up on some of mine back in Chapter 1?

"I felt like I had scarlet letters branded on me spelling out the word FIRED. Even if I wanted to get another corporate job, which I wasn't sure I did, would they even hire me if they checked and saw that I had been involuntarily terminated from my last job?"

This brought up emotional baggage around shame, unworthiness, not "enoughness," among others.

My limiting belief was that no one would want to hire me if they knew I got fired from my last job. That couldn't be further from the truth!

Here's the thing: Limiting beliefs aren't facts. They're just thoughts—thoughts that we've repeated so often that they've become ingrained in our subconscious mind. And because they're just thoughts, they can be changed.

Research indicates that as much as **95 percent of our cognition takes place in the subconscious mind**, meaning that most of our daily decisions and leadership behaviors are shaped by mental patterns and beliefs outside our conscious awareness.[12]

As Henry Ford famously said, "Whether you think you can, or you think you can't, you're right." Your beliefs shape your reality. If you believe you're not good enough, you'll find evidence to support that belief. If you believe you're capable of achieving great things, you'll find a way to make it happen.

That's why it's so important to identify and challenge your limiting beliefs. Because until you do, they'll continue to hold you back from creating the life you truly want.

The Impact of Limiting Beliefs

Limiting beliefs don't just live in your head—they show up in your actions, your relationships, and your career.

---

12 Amanda Reill, "A Simple Way to Make Better Decisions," *Harvard Business Review*, December 5, 2023, https://hbr.org/2023/12/a-simple-way-to-make-better-decisions.

For example:

- A **fear of failure** might stop you from applying for a promotion or starting your own business.

- A **scarcity mindset** might make you settle for a lower salary or avoid investing in yourself.

- A belief that you're **not good enough** might lead you to overwork, burn out, or stay in toxic environments because you don't believe you deserve better.

My Personal Struggles with Limiting Beliefs

For me, limiting beliefs have been one of the biggest obstacles I've had to overcome. Even now, as I work toward building a successful business as an author, speaker, educator, and coach, I still find myself wrestling with thoughts like:

- *It will take me a long time to make money at this—if I ever do.*

- *Who am I to do this?*

- *Why would someone pay me to do XYZ?*

- *My messaging is too diluted, and I have too many interests.*

- *There are already people doing what I want to be doing.*

- *What if I get too big and am seen too much, and it ruins my relationships?*

- *What if I fail, and I've been out of marketing for so long that I've become irrelevant if I ever want to transition back into a marketing leadership role?*

- *What if I say the wrong thing during an interview or onstage, and people think I'm stupid, rude, or XYZ—and I get canceled?*

These thoughts can be paralyzing, but I've learned that the first step to overcoming them is to acknowledge them. Once I name my limiting beliefs, I can start to challenge them and replace them with more empowering thoughts.

For example, when I catch myself thinking, *Who am I to do this?* I remind myself that I have a unique story, perspective, and set of skills that no one else has. There's room for me in this space, and my voice matters.

You think the scarlet letter limiting belief was my only one? Wrong. I've struggled with limiting beliefs throughout my life and career, and many of them can be traced back to my early experiences. Shame was a common theme I uncovered as I went through my self-assessment and examination process.

Growing up, I carried a lot of shame. My mom was on welfare for a significant part of my childhood, and I was often embarrassed by the provocative way she dressed and acted. She drove an old junker car, and when she dropped me off at my rich friends' houses, I felt like I wanted to disappear. In fact, I was so ashamed that I would wait outside while she paid for groceries with a book of food stamps because I couldn't bear to be seen.

That shame followed me everywhere. It made me feel unworthy, like I didn't belong.

Here's another example. In grade school, I had the opportunity to join several gifted classes, but I was too afraid to take the leap. I was terrified of being the dumbest person in the class, of failing and proving to everyone that I didn't belong there. So, I stayed where I was comfortable, even though I knew, and my teachers knew, I was capable of more.

Another one of those painful shame memories is from when I'd spend weekends with my grandparents when my mom wanted to go out partying. On Sundays, I would go to Catholic mass with my grandparents. I was baptized but hadn't been confirmed, so when it was time for communion, I had to sit alone in the pews while my grandparents and the other kids my age went up to receive the Eucharist. I felt so unworthy, so out of place. Like a dirty heathen outsider. Also, why didn't my grandparents just allow me to walk up beside them and allow the priest to give me a blessing instead of abandoning me in the pews to feel like a leper? I chalk it up to the era. The eighties and nineties were a helluva time to be alive as a kid!

These experiences as well as many others—maybe those will go into book 2—shaped my beliefs about myself, my worth, and what I was capable of. They limited me by making me afraid to take risks, afraid to be seen, and afraid to fail.

It took me decades to realize that limiting beliefs are not permanent. They can be identified, challenged, and replaced with empowering beliefs that support your growth and success. And I bet you have some of your own stories like that. And just like I did, you can identify and challenge them too.

Strategies for Identifying Limiting Beliefs

Identifying your limiting beliefs is the first step to overcoming them. Here are some strategies that I found to be helpful:

1. Journaling Prompts

- What do I believe about myself?

- What do I believe about success, money, or relationships?

- What am I most afraid of?

- What's the worst thing that could happen if I fail?

2. Pay Attention to Your Inner Critic

- Notice the negative thoughts that pop into your head throughout the day. What are they telling you?

3. Reflect on Your Childhood

- What messages did you receive about yourself, others, and the world before the age of seven?

- How might those messages still be influencing you today?

Understanding and Overcoming Fear Programs

Like limiting beliefs, fear is one of the biggest obstacles that holds people back. It can show up in many forms, from the fear of failure to the fear of judgment to the fear of change.

Fear is a natural human emotion that serves an important purpose: to protect us from harm. But sometimes, our fears can become irrational and hold us back from living our best lives.

Some common roots of fear include:

- **Fear of the Unknown:** The uncertainty of what lies ahead can be scary.

- **Fear of Failure:** The possibility of not succeeding can be paralyzing.

- **Fear of Loss:** The potential loss of something valuable (e.g., a job, a relationship, a sense of security) can be devastating.

These fears can manifest in different areas of life. For example, you might fear changing careers because you're afraid of the unknown or because you're afraid of failing. Or you might fear ending a relationship because you're afraid of being alone or because you're afraid of losing the comfort and security it provides.

One of my biggest fears was the fear of failure. After I was fired, I worried that I wouldn't be able to rebuild my career or create a life I loved. I felt a deep sense of shame and stigma around being fired, and it took me a long time to reframe and reprogram that experience. What I discovered, though, is that fear often loses its power when we face it head-on.

Stories of Others Overcoming Fear Help Us Do the Same

One of my mentors shared her own story of being fired and how it ultimately became a turning point in her life. She reminded me that being fired wasn't a reflection of my worth or abilities—it was an opportunity to realign with my purpose.

Reading Tim Ferriss's *The 4-Hour Workweek* also helped me shift my perspective. He wrote:

> *"I have quit three jobs and have been fired from most of the rest. Getting fired, despite sometimes coming as a surprise and leaving you scrambling, is often a Godsend. Someone else makes the decision for you, and it's impossible to sit in the wrong job for the rest of your life. Most people aren't*

lucky enough to get fired and die a slow, spiritual death over thirty to forty years of tolerating the mediocre." [13]

That quote hit me like a lightning bolt. It helped me see that being fired wasn't the end of the road—it was a new beginning.

Our Fear of Change

Change is the only constant in life. Whether it's a career shift, a relationship change, or a personal transformation, change is inevitable. And while some people embrace change with open arms, others fear it and resist it at every turn.

The truth is, fearing change can hold you back from growth, fulfillment, and living your best life. It can keep you stuck in your comfort zone, prevent you from pursuing your dreams, and limit your potential.

But here's the good news: You can learn to overcome your fear of change. You can develop resilience, adaptability, and a growth mindset that allows you to embrace change as an opportunity for growth and transformation.

To recap:

- **Reprogramming** is the strategy session: deciding what messages you want to send out to the world (and yourself).

- Reprogramming changes your *beliefs*.

---

[13] Timothy Ferriss, *The 4-Hour Workweek: Escape 9–5, Live Anywhere, and Join the New Rich* (Expanded and Updated Edition; New York: Crown, 2009), 51.

Reprogramming means identifying fears and catching negative thoughts, questioning their truth, and replacing them with more empowering thoughts.

CALL TO ACTION

IF YOU HAVE **THE REBRAND YOU COMPANION WORKBOOK,** HEAD TO THE SECTION OF THE CORRESPONDING CHAPTER AND COMPLETE THE ASSOCIATED QUESTIONS AND PROMPTS.

Now it's your turn! It's time to identify your limiting beliefs and uncover your fears.

Identify Your Limiting Beliefs

- List out the areas of your life where you feel stuck—career, relationships, health, money.

- For each area, write down the beliefs you hold.

- Are they supportive or limiting?

- For every limiting belief, write a new, empowering belief to replace it.

- Repeat these new beliefs daily—out loud, in your journal, or even on sticky notes around your house.

Uncover Your Fears

- Write down what you're afraid of and why.

- Is there evidence of other people overcoming a similar fear?

- What is the worst possible scenario tied to your fear?

- How does it feel naming your fear?

- What could a worst-case-scenario contingency and response plan look like for you?

Now that you understand how to reframe your perspective and reprogram limiting beliefs and fears, we're going to talk about how to rewire your brain and create new patterns and habits that get rid of the old baggage and set you up for success with your new rebrand concept!

Remember this: Reframing gives you a new perspective. Reprogramming gives you a new script. And, in Chapter 11, we'll discuss how rewiring makes it your new reality.

CHAPTER 11

Rewire—Make it Stick

Even if you've never explored personal development—though that seems unlikely if you're reading this book—you've probably heard of *The Secret* and the Law of Attraction.

Author Rhonda Byrne's book *The Secret,* along with the movie that followed, brought the Law of Attraction into mainstream awareness.[14] Many well-known figures, including Oprah and various A-list celebrities, support its principles and claim to have experienced its power.

The Law of Attraction is the idea that your thoughts and feelings act as magnets, attracting experiences, people, and opportunities that align with your energy. This brings us to a related word you've likely encountered frequently over the last decade: manifestation.

While these two concepts are connected, they are distinct. Here's the difference:

Law of Attraction: This universal principle (according to the spiritual community—though it is still debated in the quantum science community) states that "like attracts like." It suggests that your thoughts, feelings, beliefs, and actions produce vibrations that draw similar experiences into your life. Many in the spiritual community view this concept as a fundamental law of the universe—basically like

---

14 Rhonda Byrne, *The Secret* (New York: Atria Books, 2006).

the science community accepts gravity as a foundational principal to "how things work."

Manifestation: This is the process of consciously creating your desired reality through focused thought, intention, and action. It involves actively using the Law of Attraction to transform your goals and desires into tangible outcomes. Remember back in Chapter 6 when you visualized your ideal life and created a vision board? You were actively manifesting your desired reality.

In simple terms:

The Law of Attraction = passive. It's the underlying principle that makes manifestation possible.

Manifestation = active. It's the intentional practice of applying the Law of Attraction to achieve specific outcomes.

Regardless of whether you're a skeptic or a believer, there's no denying that the concept of manifestation has become a cultural phenomenon. But what lies beneath the surface? Is it simply wishful thinking, or is there genuine science (and strategy) behind creating the rebranded life you desire? I'm pretty sure you can guess which side of the spectrum my beliefs are on.

So, now that you've reframed your perspective and reprogrammed your beliefs, we arrive at the crucial step that most people overlook: **rewiring**. This is where you create and establish new thoughts and beliefs as habits, effectively changing the pathways in your brain.

Science calls this neuroplasticity. I call it fascinating.

Neuroplasticity: Your Brain's Built-In Rebrand Button

Let's start with the science, because I know some of you still have some doubts, consider what I just wrote as woo-woo, and want the receipts. You want proof. I get it. I respect it.

The *Concise Medical Dictionary* defines neuroplasticity as, "the ability of the brain to develop new neurons and/or new synapses in response to stimulation and learning."[15] Put simply, neuroplasticity is your brain's ability to change and rewire itself throughout your life.

Think of your brain like software or the apps on your phone. Your apps are continually being updated with new versions and releases that incorporate new features and bug fixes. Your brain works in the same way. It's always updating its software based on what you think, feel, and do.

According to the *Journal of Neuroscience,* genetic, environmental, experiential, and lifestyle factors influence neuroplasticity, including:[16]

- **Sensory and Motor Experience:** Changes in sensory and motor input, like learning new skills or exploring new environments, can lead to structural and functional changes in the brain.

- **Learning and Practice:** Repeated engagement in tasks and learning new information strengthens neural connections and promotes neuroplasticity.

- **Hormones:** Hormonal fluctuations, such as those associated with puberty and aging, can impact brain development and plasticity.

- **Stress:** Chronic stress can negatively affect neuroplasticity, while appropriate levels of stress can also trigger it.

---

15 "Neuroplasticity," in *Concise Medical Dictionary, Oxford Reference,* accessed August 3, 2025, https://www.oxfordreference.com/view/10.1093/oi/authority.20110803100230276.

16 Rachel G. H. Brans et al., "Brain Plasticity and Intellectual Ability Are Influenced by Shared Genes," *Journal of Neuroscience* 30, no. 16 (2010): 5519–5524, https://doi.org/10.1523/JNEUROSCI.5841-09.2010.

- **Environmental Factors:** The environment, including social interactions, can significantly influence brain development and plasticity.

- **Diet and Exercise:** Nutrient-rich diets and regular physical activity can positively impact brain health and neuroplasticity.

- **Neurotransmitters and Growth Factors:** These chemicals play a crucial role in regulating neural communication and promoting neuroplasticity.

- **Drugs and Medications:** Certain drugs can alter brain activity and influence neuroplasticity, while some medications can be used to promote it.

- **Sleep:** Adequate sleep is essential for consolidating memories and supporting neuroplasticity.

- **Aging:** Neuroplasticity is a lifelong process, but its capacity can be influenced by age, with some aspects being more pronounced during specific developmental periods.

- **Genetic Factors:** Individual differences in genes can impact an individual's capacity for neuroplasticity.

Let me distill some of the scientific literature down with a real-life example you can relate to. Have you ever noticed how much easier it was to learn new things when you were younger? I sure do. When I was a little girl, I took piano lessons up until the time I ran out of keys on my limited keyboard to practice. Because my mom never wanted to ask my father for anything after their divorce and because I was too young and intimidated by my father to ask him for an "expensive" item like a new Casio keyboard that had eighty-eight keys, I never got a new keyboard, which meant I didn't have a way to practice more advanced lessons. So, I quit.

One of my bucket list items was always to play the piano again. I love classical piano music. So, I bought a piano a few years ago. During COVID, I thought I'd have more time to learn and play. So, I ended up hiring a woman to come to my house and teach me. After only a few lessons, I realized how much harder it was to learn to play the piano as an adult. It felt like it came naturally to me as a kid. Layer on top of that a different style of teaching and curriculum, it felt like what I imagine Millennial or Gen X parents trying to do Common Core math with their kids feel like. When my dog unfortunately died a few short weeks after I began piano lessons and the pressure of trying to practice in between lessons became too much, I burst out crying during a lesson one day when I couldn't quite get the hang of a few keys—and that was the end of my adult piano lessons.

It is harder to learn new things as an adult because of neuroplasticity. But, don't get it twisted, my friend. It's harder, but it's not impossible. There's still hope for us elders. The reality is, it's way easier to learn new things when we're kids because our brains are different in our early years. I'm not mad that I bought my piano because it looks beautiful in my living room LOL, and I know some day, I'll probably pick it up again and do the DIY online lessons.

More Scientists and Doctors Link the Law of Attraction to Quantum Physics

If you're reading this book, there's a very good chance you've heard of Dr. Joe Dispenza. Joe Dispenza is a well-known author, speaker, and educator who focuses on the intersection of neuroscience, epigenetics, and quantum physics as they relate to personal transformation and healing. He is best known for his books such as *Breaking the Habit of Being Yourself, You Are the Placebo,* and *Becoming Supernatural.* Dispenza teaches that by changing your thoughts and emotions, you can rewire your brain, change your biology, and create profound changes in your life.

He gained initial public attention after appearing in the 2004 film *What the Bleep Do We Know!?,* which explored the connection between science and spirituality. Since then, he has built a global following through workshops, retreats, and online courses, where he guides people through meditation and mental exercises designed to help them break old habits, heal from illness, and manifest new realities.

Dispenza's work is sometimes met with skepticism from the mainstream scientific community, as some of his claims about quantum physics and healing are still considered controversial or lacking in rigorous scientific evidence. (I doubt they will be considered controversial much longer.) Regardless, many people report positive personal transformations after applying his teachings.

But you know what's really exciting to me? More left-brained, highly credentialed people like neurosurgeons and scientists have been coming out and talking about new research that connects the woo-woo stuff Dispenza talks about with freaking scientific, substantiated evidence. One of those people was Dr. James Doty, a neuroscientist who appeared on several of my favorite podcasts like Lewis Howes's *The School of Greatness* and *The Mel Robbins Show.*

One of the best books I read last year was *Mind Magic* by James R. Doty, MD. It explains how our thoughts and intentions literally sculpt the neural pathways in our brains.[17] Dispenza's research takes it further, showing that when you combine intention (what you want) with elevated emotion (how you feel), you create new neural networks

---

17 James R. Doty, *Mind Magic: The Neuroscience of Manifestation and How It Changes Everything* (New York: Avery, 2023).

that support your new identity. In other words: You can teach your old brain new tricks, and those tricks can change your life.

Energy, Frequency, and the Law of Attraction

Now, let's get a little woo—stay with me, because this is where the magic happens. Albert Einstein is often quoted as saying, "Energy cannot be created or destroyed; it can only be changed from one form to another." And neuroscientists like Dr. Bruce Lipton have proven that thoughts and emotions are forms of energy. Every thought you think, every feeling you feel, is sending out a frequency—like a radio signal—into the universe.

Esther and Jerry Hicks, in *The Vortex,* teach that everything is responding to you and the way you feel.[18] The Law of Attraction is simple: Like attracts like. High-vibe energy (love, joy, appreciation) attracts more of the same. Low-vibe energy (fear, anger, resentment) brings more of that too. So what? Well, you have the choice to tune your frequency to match the life you want. And, yes, it's a choice.

Manifestation: Turning Thought into Reality

Manifestation is the process of turning your thoughts, feelings, and beliefs into tangible reality. It's not just about daydreaming or making a wish—true manifestation requires you to align your energy, mindset, and actions with your desired outcome. Neuroscientists have shown that focused attention and repeated practice can change the brain through neuroplasticity, and many propose that combining intention,

---

18 Esther Hicks and Jerry Hicks, *The Vortex: Where the Law of Attraction Assembles All Cooperative Relationships* (Carlsbad, CA: Hay House, 2009).

emotion, and action can help rewire your brain and shift your energetic state. Dispenza, a frequent speaker on the topic, explains that when you consistently focus on what you want, feel the emotions of already having it, and take inspired action, you literally rewire your brain and shift your energetic frequency. This alignment creates a powerful feedback loop: The more you believe and feel as if your vision is real, the more you attract circumstances that match that vibration. Manifestation is both an art and a science, blending intention, emotion, and action to bring your dreams into the physical world.

Why Feeling Good Is Not Optional—It's Essential

While feeling good is essential, we also need to be realistic. None of us "feel good" all the time. Life can throw some truly awful curveballs, things you never asked for and definitely do not deserve. Maybe you are dealing with a health crisis, a loss, or a situation that is completely out of your control. If you are feeling frustrated, angry, or just plain exhausted, please know that those feelings are valid. You are not failing at life, and you are not doing anything wrong by having a very human response to a hard situation.

You do not have to force yourself to smile or pretend everything is fine when it is not. Give yourself permission to feel what you feel, and when you are ready, gently reach for even the smallest bit of relief or hope. Sometimes, feeling good simply means feeling a little less bad, or finding one thing, no matter how tiny, that brings you comfort or peace in the moment.

Trying to hustle your way through low energy or negative emotions will not create the life you want. Even the most strategic plan will fall flat if you are not energetically aligned with your vision.

Feeling good isn't just a nice-to-have; it's the foundation of your new life design. When you feel good, you're in alignment with your authentic self and your desires. You become a magnet for opportunities, people, and experiences that match your high-vibe energy. This idea isn't just spiritual fluff. Quantum physics shows that everything in the universe, including you, is made of energy vibrating at different frequencies. To attract what you want, you need to meet it at its frequency.

Wherever you are right now, be gentle with yourself. Progress is not about perfection or constant positivity. It is about honoring your experience, taking care of your heart, and moving forward at your own pace. Your goal is simply to do what's within your control to find positivity and higher-vibrational thoughts and feelings.

How Do You Know What Frequency You're On?

Great question. You can't raise your vibration if you don't know your baseline, or what the "frequency" of your dream life even is. Here's how to figure it out:

Check in with your feelings. Your emotions are your internal GPS. When you feel good—excited, grateful, inspired—you're vibrating high. When you feel bad—anxious, angry, hopeless—you're vibrating low.

Notice your results. What are you attracting? If your life feels like a series of unfortunate events, it's time to tune up your frequency.

Get clear on what you want. What does your dream life feel like? Confident? Free? Abundant? That's the frequency you need to embody now, before the external results show up.

Cymatic Frequency: The Power of Words and Sound

Let's get even more tangible. Cymatics is the study of visible sound and vibration. Billy Carson and other researchers have shown that sound frequencies can literally change physical matter. Think of the famous water experiments conducted by Dr. Masaru Emoto. In his book, *The Hidden Messages in Water,*[19] he explains that when positive words or music are played to water, the molecules form beautiful, harmonious patterns. And when negative words were spoken, the molecule patterns became chaotic, ugly and distorted.

Your words are spells. When you say, "I'm broke," you're not just describing your bank account—you're speaking that reality into existence. The vibrations created by your thoughts and words ripple out, shaping your reality. Want to alter your reality? Start with the words you speak and the thoughts you think.

You don't have to be high-vibe 24/7 (spoiler: No one is). But the more you practice, the easier it gets to shift back into positive alignment when life throws you curveballs.

Affirmations and the Power of Words

Affirmations are positive statements that you repeat to yourself, often with the intention of shifting your mindset and beliefs. What's really fascinating is that they're more than just feel-good phrases. When practiced consistently, affirmations can help rewire your brain by creating new neural pathways. As Dr. Norman Doidge describes in *The*

---

19 Masaru Emoto, *The Hidden Messages in Water* (New York: Atria Books, 2004).

Brain That Changes Itself[20], the brain is capable of forming new connections throughout life, and practices like affirmations can play a role in this process.

You might remember from earlier in the book that Neuro-Linguistic Programming (NLP) also highlights the power of language and thought patterns. NLP shows us that the words we use and the beliefs we hold can shape our behaviors and the results we experience in life.

When you use affirmations, you are training your mind to focus on what you want to become, rather than what you fear or want to avoid. For example, instead of saying, "I am always stressed," you might say, "I am the type of person capable of handling challenges with calm and confidence." Over time, your brain begins to accept these new beliefs as reality, which can lead to real changes in your actions and results.

Writing your own affirmations is a powerful exercise. Choose statements that reflect the qualities, habits, or outcomes you want to embody. Make them present tense, personal, and positive. For example:

- I am the type of person who follows through on my goals.

- I am open to new opportunities and growth.

- I am worthy of success and happiness.

Affirmations are not just a one-time activity. They will become a key part of your strategic plan as you rebrand yourself. By practicing them regularly, you will strengthen your mindset, build resilience, and create a foundation for lasting change.

---

20 Norman Doidge, *The Brain That Changes Itself: Stories of Personal Triumph from the Frontiers of Brain Science* (New York: Viking, 2007).

Why This Matters for Your Rebrand

You're not just changing your LinkedIn headline or your wardrobe—you're redesigning your life from the inside out. To activate your new strategy, you have to become the person who already lives that life. That means thinking, feeling, and acting as if your vision is already real. When you do, you'll find that the right people, opportunities, and resources show up—almost like magic.

But it's not magic. It's you, harnessing the science of neuroplasticity, the power of energy and frequency, and the wisdom of your own emotions to create a life that's truly aligned with who you are and what you want.

So, as you move forward with your rebrand, remember: Your vibe is a key part of your strategy. Feel good, think good, speak good—and launch your new rebrand campaign (aka life) into action. You are a powerful creator. Your thoughts, feelings, and words are not just "nice ideas"—they are the building blocks of your reality. Raise your vibration, align with your vision, and become the energetic match for the life you desire. God, Source, the Universe (and your brain) will do the rest.

CALL TO ACTION

IF YOU HAVE *THE REBRAND YOU COMPANION WORKBOOK,* HEAD TO THE SECTION OF THE CORRESPONDING CHAPTER AND COMPLETE THE ASSOCIATED QUESTIONS AND PROMPTS.

Write three to five affirmation statements that reflect the qualities, habits, or outcomes you want to embody. Make them present tense, personal, and positive.

You've learned the science. You've explored the woo. Now it's time to bridge the gap between knowing and becoming. So, how do you actually raise your vibration and align with your new life design? Set an intention each day to focus on the key pillars of your vitality. Strive for consistency. You're not going to get it perfect every day, so give yourself some grace.

- **Physical:** Move your body, eat nourishing food, get enough sleep. Your body is your frequency transmitter.

- **Emotional:** Process your feelings, don't suppress them. Practice gratitude and forgiveness.

- **Mental:** Feed your mind with positive, empowering thoughts. Limit exposure to negativity (yes, that includes doomscrolling).

- **Social:** Surround yourself with high-vibe people. Distance yourself from energy vampires.

- **Spiritual:** Meditate, pray, spend time in nature—whatever connects you to something bigger.

We're heading to a new section next. It's time to activate, my friend! See you in Chapter 12!

STEP 5

R

E

B

R

Activate Your Aligned Strategy

N

D

CHAPTER 12

Focus on Your "Why" and Values

New section, who dis? It's soon-to-be rebranded you, that's who! Heeeeyyyyyyyyyyyy!

Before you start mapping out your next big move, let's have a heart-to-heart. You know how I told you in marketing, we never launch a campaign without a reason? No one says, "Let's just throw some money at ads and see what happens!" (Well, not if they want to keep their job.) We start with the "why." Why does this campaign matter? Why should anyone care? Why are we even doing this? You know, that whole challenge and objective thing we discussed earlier?

Cool, now that we've level set on that *visibly air gags at the business cliché—like a Llyod Christmas in *Dumb and Dumber* when he realizes his best friend Harry Dunne went on a date with his crush Mary Swanson* You get it. And for my Gen Z readers, please go watch my favorite comedy movie of all time. Thanks. Let me know what you think. Fun fact: I just learned one of my new friends was an extra in that movie! A-MAZING!

OK, silliness aside. Let's flip the script to your rebranding campaign: *Why* are you doing what you're doing? *Why* are you chasing that goal, that job, that relationship, that version of yourself? If you don't know, you're just spinning your wheels. And I don't want that for you. I want you to feel lit up, not burned out. This is why (see what I did there?) your why and your values need to be at the forefront of everything before we get into strategy and tactics in the next chapter. And, if "what's your why" is starting to feel trite these days, call it whatever you want (core motivation, purpose, guiding principle, legacy). Regardless of the label, the meaning behind it is the deep, personal reason that gives your life and work meaning beyond just tasks or achievements.

You did a lot of this work back in Steps 1 and 2. So, take some time to reflect on your core values. If you haven't done the deep work on that yet, I'm going to give you a refresher and emphasize why this matters now.

The "Why" Is Your North Star

I'm going to let you in on a little secret: The most successful brands (and the happiest people) are the ones who know their why. It's not about being the loudest in the room or having the flashiest logo. It's about having a reason that gets you out of bed, even on the days when you'd rather hide under the covers and binge-watch your favorite show.

I learned this the hard way. Early in my career, I was the queen of "Sure, I'll do it!"—taking on projects just because someone asked. And for my Millennial and Gen X people who were also obsessed with *Don't Tell Mom the Babysitter's Dead* starring the lovely Christina Applegate, I was giving "I'm right on top of that, Rose!" vibes—so hard. Luckily, I did end up having a boss named Rose in my career, so that was a fun one to get to use IRL!

Anyway, did I care about half of these projects? Not really. Did I feel fulfilled? Not even close. It wasn't until I started asking, "Why does this matter? Why am I saying yes?" that things started to click. Suddenly, I wasn't just busy—I was building something that meant something. I don't think enough professionals take the time to connect how and why the work and projects they're doing support a larger vision and strategy. I implore you: Ask your leadership team. One: It'll show you're engaged. Two: You'll be like "OK, this is annoying, but I see how this fits into the bigger picture." ... Or three: "You people are all freaking clueless; how is this company even in the black right now. OMG."

Your "Why" Versus Your Values

Quick detour, because I know someone's about to get these twisted. As we covered earlier, label your why whatever resonates with you. The point is your why is your purpose. It's the big, juicy reason you're here. It's a deeply personal motivation that gives meaning to your life.

Your values are the nonnegotiables, the rules you live by. Think of your why as the destination and your values as the GPS settings that keep you on the right road.

To clear things up:

- **Why:** The impact you want to make. The legacy you want to leave.

- **Values:** The principles that guide your choices, big and small.

You need both. Otherwise, you're either lost (no why) or driving in circles (no values).

The Tony Robbins Moment (But Make It You)

Tony Robbins loves to talk about the power of your why. And he's not wrong. But you don't need to walk on hot coals to figure this out. You just need to get honest with yourself. What fires you up? What makes you want to Jersey Shore–fist pump in triumph? What would you fight for, even if no one was watching?

Quick Exercise: The Why Lightning Round
Grab a pen. (Yes, right now. I'll wait.)

- What are you passionate about, the thing you can't stop talking about?

- What pisses you off about the world and makes you want to fix it?

- What do people thank you for?

- What would you do for free, just because it feels right?

- What do you want people to say about you when you're not in the room?

Write. Don't overthink. Just let it spill.

Now, look for the patterns. That's your why, waving at you from the page.

My Example: Doing the Why Lightning Round
Here's how I answered these questions for myself:

- **What am I passionate about?** I am obsessed with intentional living, life design, and the power we have to change our reality. I can't stop talking about how our minds shape our lives, the breakthroughs in neuroscience and quantum fields, and the stories of people who come back from the edge with a new understanding that everything, absolutely everything, comes back to love. That's what keeps me up at night and gets me out of bed in the morning.

- **What pisses me off?** It pisses me off that so many people are stuck living "mid" lives—feeling trapped in jobs, relationships, or towns that drain them, silently suffering and losing hope. It breaks my heart to see people give up on themselves or spiral so far down that they lose relationships, health, or even their lives. I get angry at how unfair workplaces can be, how people are treated like numbers, and how much power we give away to systems that don't care about us.

- **What do people thank me for?** People thank me for seeing their potential when they can't see it themselves. They thank me for helping them tap into their strengths, for showing them a path forward, and for making them laugh when life feels heavy. They thank me for keeping it real and reminding them that they are powerful, even when they forget.

- **What would I do for free?** Help connect people to what's possible. Nothing lights me up more than seeing someone's eyes spark with hope when they realize they actually can go after that secret dream. I live for those moments when someone realizes they can change their mindset and way they've been approaching life. When they finally believe in themselves, step into their power, and start building a life and career that feels true.

- **What do I want people to say about me?** I want people to say I brought energy, courage, and realness. I want them to say I helped them see how amazing they are, that I inspired them to take action even when they were scared, and that I reminded them of their own power. I hope they say, "She did it scared, so I can too." I want to be remembered as someone who helped others rebrand their lives, own their gifts, and step into a higher version of themselves, all with love at the center.

When I look at my answers, I see a clear theme: I want to empower people to realize their potential, live with intention, and create lives that feel authentic and joyful.

Crafting Your "Why" Statement (No Corporate Jargon Allowed)

Now it's your turn. Take a look at your own answers. Circle or highlight the words and ideas that show up more than once or feel especially important. These are clues to your core motivation. This isn't for a LinkedIn headline. This is for you. Make it simple, make it true, make it something you'd actually say out loud.

To help you shape your why statement, use this simple formula: "To [verb] [who/what] so that [impact]."

Examples:

- To empower people to own their voices so that they can change the world.

- To create spaces where people feel seen and heard.

- To make complicated things simple, so people can live better.

If it makes you smile (or tear up a little), you're on the right track.

Here's mine: *"To empower people and organizations to reach their full potential so they can be happier and achieve big goals."*

This is why I'm writing this book. *YOU* are my why.

If you feel stuck, try reading your answers out loud or sharing them with a friend. Sometimes, hearing yourself say it helps the real why come forward. Remember, this is for you. There are no wrong answers.

Take your time, and trust that your why will become clearer the more you reflect.

Living Your "Why"
(Because Otherwise, What's the Point?)

Do you see how powerful that free-flow brain dump was? That was visceral. That's the power of journaling. But now, it's back to you.

Here's where most people mess up: They write a beautiful why statement and then ... nothing changes. But not you. You're going to use your why as a filter for every decision, every opportunity, every *"should I or shouldn't I?"* moment.

Ask yourself:

- Does this align with my why?

- Am I living my values or just talking about them?

- If I say yes to this, am I moving closer to my purpose or further away?

Obviously, there are some things we have to say yes to (like paying taxes, taking out the trash, and unsexy stuff like that). But when it comes to other areas you have personal agency over making a choice about (use your discernment), keep this in mind: If it's not a hell yes, it's a no. (Or at least a "not right now.")

Values: Your Nonnegotiables

Zero flexibility on this one. Your values are the things you won't compromise on, no matter how shiny the opportunity. If your life was a brand, these would be your brand pillars. These are the principles that guide your decisions, actions, and beliefs. They're the things that are most important to you in life.

You already did this work in Step 1, so take a moment to revisit your list. Remind yourself of your top values and notice if anything has shifted for you since then. If you want a quick refresher, here are some examples: integrity, freedom, connection, growth, creativity, service, balance, adventure, authenticity, and impact.

Now, reaffirm your top three. These are your ride or dies. The things you'll protect, even if it means saying no to something good in favor of something great.

Aligning Your Goals with Your "Why" and Values

If your goals don't line up with your why and your values, you're building a house on sand. Sure, it might look pretty for a while, but eventually, it'll sink. Research backs this—people who chase goals that aren't rooted in their values end up stressed, burned out, and wondering why they're so damn tired all the time.

But when your goals are built on your why and values? That's when the magic happens. You feel energized, focused, and happy (when all of the other stuff is aligned, which we'll talk more about in the next chapters).

I used to think my why was "to climb the ladder and make bank." After doing the work and reflecting, I know WHY I was doing that, which I talked about earlier (mindset around scarcity and unworthiness and a need to feel safe.) But, as you can probably guess, that got old, fast. And I actually WASN'T safe even though I was doing EVERY-

THING you could possibly think of that would mean safety and longevity and praise for how worthy I was because of how PERFECT and HARDWORKING I was.

I feel sorry for that old version of me. And I send her so much love and grace and forgiveness. She was actually getting closer to her why as she intentionally advocated for creating her former corporate job to be about "serving the greater good" and using huge corporate budgets to make an impact and help underserved communities. She was bringing together stakeholders from across multiple industries and entertainment and influencers to shine a light on societal issues that can make all the difference in setting people up to be successful and secure in their lives. So, I was following the breadcrumbs of things that were a hell yes and sparking joy and Jersey Shore–style fist pumps, but it wasn't quite it. As one of the psychics I talked to told me later, the ceiling wasn't high enough where I was. I couldn't make the true impact I came on this planet to make.

I talked about light and dark earlier, which is really about polarity. You have to see the darkness in order to see the light. So, I honor that experience. Had I not been living and operating my life that way and didn't have the very sucky wake-up call of getting fired, I probably never would've done the DEEP, intentional, time-intensive work that allowed me to stop waiting to pursue a career that aligns with my TRUE why.

Now, I clearly know my why and my values. My values are freedom, impact, and authenticity. My why is to help people rebrand their lives from the inside out, so they can show up as their boldest, truest selves. My why is to help teams and leaders communicate better and be more empathetic and authentic, so they can have more fun and make a bigger impact inside and outside of their organizations.

So, if something doesn't check those boxes, said in the words of OG *American Idol* judge Randy Jackson—who I would absolutely have sign my sword if that's all I had on me at the time—it's a no for me, dawg.

Thank you, again, for indulging my movie quote references—by the way, that was from *Step Brothers* if you didn't get it.

CALL TO ACTION

IF YOU HAVE THE REBRAND YOU COMPANION WORKBOOK, HEAD TO THE SECTION OF THE CORRESPONDING CHAPTER AND COMPLETE THE ASSOCIATED QUESTIONS AND PROMPTS.

Take some time to revisit the values identification work you did in Steps 1 and 2. Look at your list of top values and ask yourself: Which ones feel most important to you right now? Why do these values matter to you? How do they show up in your daily life and decisions?

Now, take a look at the marketing concept you brainstormed. Evaluate whether your values and your why are truly reflected in it. If something feels off, use the exercises and examples in this chapter to guide your exploration and make adjustments.

- Write your why statement. Stick it somewhere you'll see it every day.

- List your top three values. These are your new decision-making filters.

- Next time you set any goal or have a decision to make, ask: Does this support my why? Does it honor my values?

If not, tweak it. Or toss it. Life's too short for shit that doesn't fit. You've done the deep work. You know your why. You know your values. Next up: We're turning that mission into a plan. Get ready to set goals that actually mean something and build a strategy that's as bold as you are. See you in the next chapter, where we turn your why into your what, your how, and your "hell yes, I did that."

CHAPTER 13

Goal Setting and Action Planning

You've done the soul-searching, the visioning, the "what if" daydreaming. You understand the huge role your mindset plays in the entire process. And you're locked in on your why and your values.

Now it's time to get real.

We're going to launch your new vision and campaign concept—the one you finalized in Chapter 7—the one you hypothesize will have the best chance of meeting your objective. This is where you turn your big, beautiful new concept and vision into a plan you can actually follow—one that doesn't just live in your head, but shows up in your calendar, your habits, and your results.

When marketers create a new go-to-market strategy, we set clear objectives, map out every step, and track progress like our bonus depends on it (because, let's be honest, it usually does). Marketers never launch a campaign without a clear plan for measuring success. They set specific objectives, define Key Performance Indicators (KPIs), and track progress over time. Marketers also use consistent reporting frameworks—weekly, monthly, quarterly, and annual reports—to assess the effectiveness of their campaigns. These reports help them figure out what's working, what's not, and where to focus their efforts moving forward.

Now, before you start spiraling like I did, NOTHING is permanent. So, leave the analysis paralysis at the door and save yourself months (ahem years!) of overthinking and trying to get everything perfect on the first pass. Because you won't get it perfect. And that's OK.

Think about it. Have you seen the same commercial from Ford, or the same ad creative from Nike since the brands first launched? No. They iterate and refine as they learn what resonates. So, don't be like me and spin your wheels trying to perfect your launch.

Could it flop? Sure. But you won't know until you try. Is your first launch likely to be a total failure? Absolutely not. Just as we did with our creative concepting, we will take elements that *are* working and continue to refine and eliminate those that aren't. You're going to learn something either way. Just like I did.

You're the CEO and CMO of your own life now. This chapter is all about turning your brainstormed ideas into clear, actionable steps. It's time to take those ideas and turn them into actionable goals using the SMART goals framework.

What Are SMART Goals?

If you've never heard of a SMART goal, bless your heart. They're used all the time in corporate for performance management. Setting SMART goals helps you stay motivated and ensures the activities you're doing align with the bigger picture and your actions align with your vision.

SMART goals are Specific, Measurable, Achievable, Relevant, and Time-bound. They're like a roadmap for your success. They give you clarity, focus, and a way to track your progress.

Here's what each element means:

- **Specific:** <u>Clearly define what you want to achieve.</u>
  Instead of saying, "I want a new career," say, "I want to transition into a project management role by gaining relevant certifications and networking with professionals in the field."

- **Measurable:** Include criteria to track your progress.
  Instead of saying, "I want to improve my skills," say, "I want to complete two professional certifications and attend three industry networking events within the next six months."

- **Achievable:** Make sure the goal is realistic and attainable.
  Instead of saying, "I want to become a CEO in two years," set a more realistic goal like "I want to secure a mid-level management position in my target industry within the next twelve months by leveraging my transferable skills and gaining additional experience."

- **Relevant:** Align the goal with your values and long-term vision.
  Make sure the goal supports your overall mission and purpose. For example, "I want to transition into a career in user experience design because it aligns with my passion for creating intuitive and impactful digital solutions."

- **Time-bound:** Set a deadline for achieving the goal.
  Instead of saying, "I want to change careers," say, "I want to secure a new role in my target industry within the next nine months by applying to at least five relevant job openings per week and tailoring my resume for each opportunity."

SMART goals take the guesswork out of goal setting and give you a clear target to aim for and a way to measure your progress along the way. While they may have been annoying AF in your current or previous job, you can use them personally to track your personal growth and make adjustments as needed. They can be like the Key Performance Indicators (KPIs) for your life.

Introducing OKRs: Another Goal Setting Framework

SMART goals not your thing? OKURRR. (See what I did thurr, I mean there.) Lots of companies use the **OKR (objectives and key results)** framework to set and measure goals.

OKRs are a simple yet powerful way to align your efforts with a larger vision.

Here are some random examples to help explain how they work:
- **Objective:** A clear, inspiring goal you want to achieve.
    - Example: Improve customer satisfaction.
- **Key Results:** Specific, measurable outcomes that indicate progress toward the objective.
    - Example: Increase Net Promoter Score (NPS) from 70 to 80 within six months.

You can also apply the OKR framework to your personal life. For example:
- **Objective:** Improve my physical health.
- **Key Results:**
    - Exercise for thirty minutes, five days a week.
    - Lose ten pounds in three months.
    - Increase my energy levels by getting seven to eight hours of sleep per night.

OKRs and SMART goals work well together. While OKRs provide a high-level vision, SMART goals break that vision into actionable steps. Because they break things down into specific steps, you can use whichever format you're most comfortable with, if you have a preference. My preference is that you try SMART goals first, but no worries if you want to keep things more high-level now with an OKR format.

#TeamSMARTGoals
I know, I know. You probably just puked a little in your mouth. *SMART goals? Really?*

Ugh, I know. But hear me out. Vague goals get vague results. This framework forces you to get clear, get honest, and get moving. Applying it through the lens of what YOU want is way more fun compared to creating SMART goals to align with your micromanaging boss's departmental SMART goals and feeling clueless because the company hasn't even set the enterprise-wide strategic goals yet, and you have no idea what budget you have to even plan your strategy. I definitely do NOT miss that!

Let's examine how we can utilize SMART goals for a person seeking a new job.

Basic Goal: I want a new job.

SMART Goal: I will apply to three new roles in my desired field each week and land a new position by September 1.

See the difference?

One is a wish; the other is a plan. Also, if you recall from the last chapter, where we discussed quantum theory and manifestation, the more specific you are, the easier it is for the Universe to arrange things to make it happen for you. Ask, and ye shall receive.

Told you this is way more fun than the corporate SMART goals! I'm sticking my tongue out at you right now. No hate, we're friends now, so I'm just teasing you a bit! Love you!

OK, convinced now? Good. Now, throw out the old baggage from corporate and limiting beliefs that SMART goals suck, and let's get into it, my friend!

Pro Tip: Make sure that you are setting your goals so that they are aligned with your values that you identified earlier in the book.

For instance, as it relates to career planning ...

- If your value is **freedom**, ensure your goal allows you to work remotely or offers other types of freedom and flexibility you need.

- If your value is **connection**, your goal might be to find opportunities that offer collaboration and focus on relationship building and teamwork.

- If your value is **growth**, your goal might be to find an opportunity that is prime for promotions within the company, offers tuition reimbursement, or enables you to continue developing your skills or earning certifications.

Creating a Strategic Action Plan and Tracking It

Once you have your SMART goals, break them down into bite-size actions. What needs to happen this month? This week? Today? Marketers use campaign calendars and checklists. You can use those too, or a planner, notes app, Trello board, Notion, or a sticky note on your bathroom mirror.

The point is to make your next steps so obvious you can't help but take them—and want to track them. The critical piece you need is accountability (especially if you're a solopreneur without a boss breathing down your neck, holding your feet to the fire).

Brands track metrics and adjust their campaigns. You need to do the same. Set up weekly or biweekly check-ins with yourself. Find an accountability partner, or join a group. If you're unsure about which group to join or how to find the right fit, don't worry. I'll walk you through all of that in Step 6: Network and Build Your Community.

Celebrate wins, analyze setbacks, and tweak your plan as you go. Progress, not perfection.

We're just about to wrap things up in this chapter, and I'm going to give you some homework. But before I do, because I love ya, I'm going to share my SMART goals with you as a reference, as they may be helpful when you create yours.

Let's look back at my initial challenge, objective, and final campaign concept.

Challenge: I'm unsure about the next phase of my career. I need to find a job that aligns with my purpose, values, and zone of genius. My job must enable me to earn a specific income target and make a positive impact on the world.

Objective: To design a life I love that is aligned with a new high-vibe, abundant version of myself.

Campaign Concept (My Vision): Knowledge Business Entrepreneur and Consultant / Chief Edutainment Officer and Stand-Up Storyteller

My dream is to have a successful knowledge and consulting business that educates, entertains, and empowers others. I would love to earn a living and impact millions of lives by writing, speaking, and teaching about my marketing and business expertise, NLP and mindset, life experiences, lessons, observations, and healing journey while sharing practical information and easy-to-understand/follow blueprints in a way that's fun for me and my audience. I want to be part of a movement that positively transforms business culture so people feel happier and businesses and employees thrive.

Vision Statement:
Build a thriving knowledge and consulting business that educates, entertains, and empowers millions of people, leveraging my marketing and communication expertise, comedy, NLP and continual education certifications, life lessons, and healing journey through writing, speaking, coaching, and digital products—focusing on high-impact

and passive income streams—while temporarily continuing marketing consulting for consistent income while I scale my knowledge business geared toward personal and professional development for people and organizations.

My SMART Goals and Action Steps (Staggered and Streamlined Example)

Goal 1: Continue Marketing Consulting Client Work

- **Specific:** Maintain marketing consulting client base to ensure consistent revenue.

- **Measurable:** Generate $*[Target Amount]* in consulting revenue, retain 100 percent of existing clients, and prospect new ones, as needed.

- **Achievable:** 10 hours/week.

- **Relevant:** Provides financial stability while building the knowledge business.

- **Time-bound:** Ongoing, reviewed quarterly.

Action Steps:

- Dedicate time each week to client management and project delivery.

- Proactively communicate with existing clients to identify new opportunities.

- Network and seek referrals for new consulting engagements, as needed.

- Track time and expenses to ensure profitability.

Goal 2: Establish a Strong Brand and Online Presence

- **Specific:** Define my brand, launch a website, and set up social media profiles.

- **Measurable:** Website live, grow followers 500+

- **Achievable:** 5–10 hours/week.

- **Relevant:** Foundation for all business activities.

- **Time-bound:** Complete by December 31.

Action Steps:

- Finalize brand story, mission, and values.

- Launch new website with updated branding.

- Post on Instagram and Facebook at least once a week (it should be way more).

- Create a TikTok account and test that medium.

- Begin posting on LinkedIn again.

- Create a content strategy and grow my email list by building an engaged audience.

Goal 3: Launch and Monetize My Expertise

- **Specific:** Launch coaching, consulting, courses, and digital products.

- **Measurable:** $*[Target Amount]* revenue from knowledge business, 50+ course students, 10+ coaching/consulting clients.

- **Achievable:** 10–15 hours/week.

- **Relevant:** Generates income and validates my business.

- **Time-bound:** Consulting (ongoing), coaching (by December 2024), course (Q2), digital products (Q1).

Action Steps:

- Develop and launch a signature course.

- Offer 1:1 coaching or consulting.

- Create and sell digital products (templates, guides, workbooks).

- Set up automated sales funnels.

Goal 4: Establish Myself as a Thought Leader

- **Specific:** Speaking engagements, guest on podcasts, share thoughts on social/blog.

- **Measurable:** 3+ speaking events, 5+ podcast/guest blog appearances.

- **Achievable:** 3–5 hours/week.

- **Relevant:** Increases visibility and credibility.

- **Time-bound:** Complete by December 31.

Action Steps:

- Create signature talk(s) and speaker kit.

- Pitch for speaking at conferences/events.

- Reach out for podcast/guest blog opportunities.

- Share insights on social media and blog.

Goal 5: Publish a Book

- **Specific:** Write and publish a book sharing my expertise and journey.

- **Measurable:** Complete manuscript draft, secure a publisher or self-publish, and launch the book.

- **Achievable:** 5–7 hours/week.

- **Relevant:** Establishes authority, supports values, helps more people at scale.

- **Time-bound:** Complete manuscript by June 2025, publish by January 2026.

Action Steps:

- Research publishing options.

- Attend writing retreat.

- Outline book chapters.

- Set weekly writing goals.

- Hire editor, designer, project manager/book launch team.

Goal 6: Invest in Health, Relationships, Continuing Education, and Fun

- **Specific:** Invest in people and things that enhance my health, wealth, intelligence, relationships, and joy.

- **Measurable:** Weekly meal prep, exercise 4–5 days/week, enroll in classes, join masterminds, and spend time with friends and family.

- **Achievable:** 10 hours/week.

- **Relevant:** Enables sustainable growth and work-life balance.

- **Time-bound:** Ongoing.

Action Steps:

- Take improv and stand-up comedy classes.

- Get certified in NLP.

- Meal prep for the week every Sunday.

- Block calendar weekday mornings for workouts.

- Research masterminds and online communities to join.

- Plan a vacation with family.

- Attend networking events to meet like-minded people.

Now, for all these goals, I need to review and update this plan monthly and my goals as needed, celebrate milestones, and stay focused on high-impact, high-leverage activities. For accountability, I'm going to make my close friends and family aware of my plans. I'm also going to hire a coach to keep me accountable. (I've spent thousands of dollars on coaches, and I would do it again in a heartbeat, and I will continue to hire coaches to support me as I grow into my higher self and need people who've been where I want to go or solve a gap or problem I have faster than I could on my own.) I want them to call me out on my bullshit when I make excuses.

OK, and because you are really growing on me, I'm going to give you one more example. But before I do, I want you to remember this:

You don't have to do it all at once! We all have different circumstances and responsibilities in our lives that can affect how much free time we have to work on our goals, like taking care of children or parents, volunteering, working multiple jobs, serving on boards, hobbies, and other commitments. Give yourself permission to take the time you need. Some goals may take months, others a year or more. Progress, not perfection! And you may even change your mind or deprioritize a goal as you are going through the process and realize you may need to make adjustments.

Don't compare yourself to me or anyone else for that matter. You may have read my goals and had a flood of anxiety. You read my personality assessment data: I can be a bit extra and overzealous about things. I also may have more time to work on things than others because I don't have children and have full agency over my schedule for the most part.

My recommendation is to start with two or three goals that feel most important and manageable for you. As you build momentum, you can add more.

Here's an example of one of my coaching client's SMART Goals

Her Vision:
Secure a fulfilling career path that aligns with personal values, leverages hard skills, and ignites passions, leading to long-term career and lifestyle goals while maintaining financial security.

Goal 1: Self-Assessment and Career Exploration

- **Specific:** Identify core values, assess hard skills, and explore potential career paths that align with passions.

- **Measurable:** Complete 3 career assessments, identify 5–7 potential career paths, and create a skills matrix.

- **Achievable:** Dedicate 3–5 hours/week to self-assessment and exploration.

- **Relevant:** Provides a foundation for targeted job searching and career development.

- **Time-bound:** Complete by January 15.

Action Steps:

- Complete career assessments (e.g., StrengthsFinder, Myers-Briggs, Values in Action).

- Reflect on past experiences to identify what energizes and motivates.

- Research potential career paths using online resources (e.g., LinkedIn, Glassdoor, industry reports).

- Create a skills map: list hard skills and see how they align with different job roles.

- Identify any skill gaps and potential training or certification opportunities.

Goal 2: Targeted Skill Development

- **Specific:** Acquire new skills or enhance existing ones to increase marketability in desired career paths.

- **Measurable:** Complete 1–2 online courses or certifications, attend 3+ workshops or webinars, and dedicate 5+ hours/week to skill development.

- **Achievable:** Focus on high-impact skills that align with target roles and career goals.

- **Relevant:** Increases confidence and competitiveness in the job market.

- **Time-bound:** Complete by March 31.

Action Steps:

- Identify key skills required for target roles.

- Enroll in online courses or certifications (e.g., Coursera, Udemy, LinkedIn Learning).

- Attend industry-specific workshops or webinars.

- Practice new skills through personal projects or volunteer work.

- Seek feedback from mentors or peers on skill development progress.

Goal 3: Networking and Informational Interviews

- **Specific:** Build connections with professionals in target industries and gather insights through informational interviews.

- **Measurable:** Connect with 20+ professionals on LinkedIn, conduct 5+ informational interviews, and attend 2+ industry events.

- **Achievable:** Leverage existing network and actively seek new connections.

- **Relevant:** Provides valuable insights and potential job leads.

- **Time-bound:** Complete by April 30, ongoing.

Action Steps:

- Update LinkedIn profile and actively connect with professionals in target industries.

- Reach out to contacts for informational interviews to learn about their roles and experiences.

- Prepare thoughtful questions for informational interviews.

- Attend industry events, conferences, or meetups.

- Follow up with contacts after informational interviews to maintain relationships.

Goal 4: Resume and Cover Letter Optimization

- **Specific:** Tailor resume and cover letter to highlight relevant skills and experiences for target roles.

- **Measurable:** Create 2–3 versions of resume and cover letter, receive feedback from career coach or mentor, and achieve a 75 percent+ application success rate.

- **Achievable:** Focus on showcasing transferable skills and accomplishments.

- **Relevant:** Increases chances of securing interviews.

- **Time-bound:** Complete by May 31.

Action Steps:

- Identify keywords and skills from target job descriptions.

- Highlight transferable skills and accomplishments in resume and cover letter.

- Quantify achievements whenever possible.

- Seek feedback from career coach, mentor, or trusted colleague.

- Tailor resume and cover letter for each job application.

Goal 5: Job Search and Interview Preparation

- **Specific:** Actively search for job openings, apply for relevant roles, and prepare for interviews.

- **Measurable:** Apply for 20+ jobs/month, secure 5+ interviews, and practice common interview questions.

- **Achievable:** Dedicate 5–10 hours/week to job searching and interview preparation.

- **Relevant:** Leads to securing a fulfilling job offer.

- **Time-bound:** Complete by June 1.

Action Steps:

- Set up job alerts on LinkedIn, Indeed, and other job boards.

- Apply for relevant job openings that align with your skills and values.

- Practice common interview questions using the STAR method.

- Conduct mock interviews with a career coach or mentor.

- Research companies and roles before each interview.

So, for accountability, she hired me to help her stay on track with her goals and to coach her through specific areas she needed support. She also informed her family about her goals, so they understood what she was striving for and would respect her boundaries if she needed to invest more time in achieving her goals and would have to decline social activities for a while. We'll be talking about that in more detail in the next chapter.

Wasn't that fun? Or did you puke in your mouth? Well, either way, it's your turn. Love you!

CALL TO ACTION

IF YOU HAVE *THE REBRAND YOU COMPANION WORKBOOK*, HEAD TO THE SECTION OF THE CORRESPONDING CHAPTER AND COMPLETE THE ASSOCIATED QUESTIONS AND PROMPTS.

Open up your Rebrand You folder, create a new document, and complete the following exercises.

1. **Start with backward planning.**
   Begin by imagining your desired long-term outcome, such as a quarterly or annual goal. Picture what success looks like at the finish line, then work backward to identify the key milestones you need to hit along the way. This approach helps you set goals that are both meaningful and achievable.

2. **Write down your top three SMART goals for the next 30, 60, 90 days (and beyond based on your unique situation).**
   Make them specific, measurable, achievable, relevant, and time-bound.

3. **Break each goal into weekly and daily actions.**
   What's the first step you can take today?

4. **Set up an accountability system.**
   Who will you check in with? How will you track your progress?

Pro Tip: If you like visual tools, try mapping this out on a Trello board, Notion, ClickUp, or a simple spreadsheet.

In the next chapter, we are going to flesh these goals out even more to ensure you have a plan so your lifestyle can adjust in support of your goals. What may you need to change in order to support achieving these goals? See you in Chapter 14: Lifestyle Design.

CHAPTER 14

Lifestyle Design

Marketers know that a brand's success isn't just about the launch; it's about managing the ecosystem that supports it. Your life is the same. You need routines, environments, and habits that make your new direction feel natural, not forced.

Now that you've got your goals and your plan, you're probably feeling pretty damn good. I love it. But if your daily life is a dumpster fire of stress, chaos, and old habits, even the best plan and your initial momentum will fizzle out. That's why we need to manage the ecosystem and establish processes that position you for success.

Remember back in Chapter 6, I asked you to envision your ideal life? What do you want your day-to-day existence to look like? How do you want to feel? How do you want to look? What do you want to spend your time doing? What will you need to do to enable that vision?

This chapter is about designing the lifestyle that matches (or works toward matching) the one you got dreamy about in Chapter 6. This is about designing areas of your life with systems and processes that will help you feel your best and motivated to take action and achieve those big, juicy goals you just set for yourself!

Categories of Life to Evaluate

When I talk about lifestyle design, I don't just mean work or health. I'm talking about the whole ecosystem. You are a multidimensional being, after all! There are lots of categories that compose your holistic life. And success in one category (or a lack of it) impacts all the other categories.

The point of doing this work is to clarify how to align your daily actions with your long-term goals and achieve balance throughout. This means making daily choices that support your goals and staying true to your values in the face of challenges or temptations. When you go through an exercise like creating SMART goals and OKRs, you have a clear plan and set of criteria that will help you know when you're living in alignment with your plan, and when you're not.

Here are the categories that make up the holistic, multidimensional awesome person you are:

- Health and fitness

- Mental and emotional well-being

- Relationships (romantic, family, friends, community)

- Career and professional growth

- Finances

- Personal growth and learning

- Spirituality or sense of purpose

- Fun, hobbies, and adventure

- Environment (your home, your workspace, your digital life)

Let's take a look at the Health and Fitness category as an example so I can show you my personal approach. And then you can tailor your own.

Health and Fitness Example:
For me, taking care of my body is essential for living a vibrant and fulfilling life. I envision myself as strong, happy, and full of energy, fueling my body with good food and consistent exercise. My purpose in this area is to avoid illness, live a long, healthy life, and have the vitality to pursue my passions and be present for those I love. Being healthy also helps me feel confident, which impacts my relationships and helps me overcome limiting beliefs.

To achieve this, my strategy includes exercising at least five days a week (with strength training three days), walking ten thousand steps daily, eating a balanced diet of whole foods with plenty of protein, minimizing processed foods and alcohol, getting seven to eight hours of quality sleep each day, and drinking a half gallon to a gallon of water each day depending on my activity level.

You don't have to overhaul everything at once. In fact, please don't! Start by picking one or two areas that feel most out of sync with your goals or values. Small, intentional changes in one area often create positive ripple effects in others. But I want you to remember: You're not always going to get it perfect (hard to hear for you perfectionists out there, I know. Same, my friend. Same). I absolutely do NOT walk ten thousand steps every day because, well, life happens, and we need to pivot and adjust as needed. But I STRIVE for moving my body and ten thousand steps. I want to hit that daily goal. But on the days I don't, I've learned to give myself grace and pick things back up the next day.

To make things easier and to position you for more days of hitting your targets than not, here are some things I've learned along the way:

- Simplify and automate where you can. The less you have to think about the basics, the more energy you have for what matters.

- Set up your environment for success. Make it easy to make good choices.

- Protect your time and energy. Boundaries are your best friend.

- Check in with yourself regularly. Are your daily actions moving you closer to your vision, or further away?

- Celebrate progress, not perfection. This is a journey, not a sprint.

- Make conscious choices. Before making a decision, ask yourself if it aligns with your values and goals.

- Practice self-care. Take care of your physical, emotional, and mental well-being.

- Seek support. Surround yourself with people who share your values and support your goals.

Lifestyle design is about creating an environment and daily rhythm that makes your goals not just possible, but probable. When your life supports your ambitions, you become unstoppable.

CALL TO ACTION

IF YOU HAVE *THE REBRAND YOU COMPANION WORKBOOK*, HEAD TO THE SECTION OF THE CORRESPONDING CHAPTER AND COMPLETE THE ASSOCIATED QUESTIONS AND PROMPTS.

Pick one or two areas of your life from the list above. For each, write a quick vision for what "great" would look like. What's one small change you could make this week to move closer to that vision? You don't have to do it all at once. Start where you are and build from there.

In the next chapter, we will delve deeper into designing your life and habits to align with your goal and for the type of person you want to become.

CHAPTER 15

Transforming Your Identity and Personal Brand

In marketing, a rebrand isn't just a new logo or a fresh color palette. It's a new story, a new promise, a new vibe. It's a company saying, "We're not who we used to be, and here's why you should care."

This chapter is about the real rebrand—the one that comes from within, defined by you and you alone, not by anything or anyone else. My goal is for you to finish this chapter with a full understanding of that. I want you to understand why the one under the surface matters more than anything else.

Can you think of a time when you or someone you know had their identity so wrapped up in something outside of themselves, it was like synonymous with who you or they were as a person? The relationship. The sport. The status. The label. The religion. The group. The company. The career. The job.

And I'm sure you can recall what often happens when that external thing you or they identified with was suddenly gone—whether or not it was by choice or uncontrollable circumstances. You feel lost. Disconnected. Like your world was flipped upside down. Like you don't know who you are anymore, why you matter, or what's next. You spent so much time building brand equity attached to this external thing, that the shock and discomfort of no longer being attached to that thing outside of yourself can full-send you into a downward spiral—I'm talking depression, existential dread, and a grade A identity crisis. You may already know this from experience or know someone in your life who had to learn this lesson the hard way—like I did.

When I got fired a week after accepting a coveted industry award at a huge conference, attending a successful experiential event I pushed for us to sponsor, receiving a substantial pay increase ready to hit my direct deposit account for the first time, and finalizing an offer letter ready to be extended to a new hire to join my team, it made me question everything about my sense of reality and who I was. I mean, this was the highest-achieving year of my career. I was so happy. I felt like I was FINALLY anointed after years of "pick me" energy and trying to prove why I was valuable. One day after I pep talked my boss after she set a meeting on my calendar to ask me for advice and tips in preparation for a panel speaking engagement she was participating in the following week—since I had been doing a lot of that public speaking myself. After I pumped her up and made her realize what a badass she is. (I honestly do think she is, and she is a sweet soul, I mean that from the bottom of my heart.) At the end of our call, she said, "Wow, I need to talk to you every morning before work! You're so motivational. Thank you!"

They FINALLY see me, I thought. *All I've wanted is to rally people and give them a "Varsity Blues" pump-up speech so we can recognize what we can accomplish together. If we lead with heart, the profit will come! They see I'm a leader and the vision I've been sharing for the last three years of why we need to invest in this area. And now I get to lead it, and I'm getting more resources and support to do it the right way!*

And along with that high, came one of the lowest lows I've ever felt—because my identity for so many years had been hinged on my association with that brand. My personal social media made it look like I was the highest-paid brand ambassador. I had more posts about that brand and the campaigns we worked on and places I traveled to work on them than posts with my own family or friends.

So, my identity was totally upended because it was so rooted in that connection. And now, in my limiting belief way of seeing the situation, I couldn't even go out on a high note. After the years of hard work, relationships built inside and outside the company, it was all gone. I was kicked out of the club. It was like I died and no one cared. Sure, there were people who reached out to me, but there were lots who I thought would—that didn't.

And that tells you everything you need to know.

Not only did I have to confront my fears and darkest shadows around shame, scarcity, worthiness, and being ostracized from my "work family" (another mouth-puke worthy expression), when I did transition to a fractional role at another company quickly after I got fired, which was an absolute blessing as I said earlier, I also realized that another part of my identity was challenged.

I'm talking Big Brand Energy (BBE). The identity that comes with working at a well-known and recognizable brand.

If you're reading this and you've ever gone from working for a large brand with a champagne budget to working for a start-up with a beer budget, you quickly realize who gives a shit about you and who likes you just for that BBE budget. Yep.

So, what's the lesson here, kids? This one deserves all caps:

Do not build your identity on top of any person or thing outside of yourself.

We'll talk about personal branding later in this chapter, and I want you to really pay attention to why you need to work on YOUR brand more than your W-2 employer's brand. Of course, share the company accolades, updates, cool projects you're working on, but diversify your portfolio, my friend. Diversify or Cry. Hmm, *takes note to check if that domain is available later*—one of the "toxic" traits I learned in my self-reflection is I buy domains for many random ideas that pop into this dome piece (what we used to call a head in the early 2000s).

Let's get one thing straight: You can't outwork your identity. You can set all the goals, buy all the planners, and download every habit tracker app in the App Store, but if you're still running the "old you" software, you'll keep getting the same old results.

OK, now that I Big Sis'd all over you, back to our regularly scheduled programming.

This is your invitation to step into the identity of the person who achieves your goals and lives your vision. This is where you become your higher self—and then show up so the world can't help but notice. You're not just changing what you do. You're changing who you are. And when you do that, everything else—your habits, your results, your reputation—shifts to match.

The Power of Identity: Who Are You Becoming?

You can't pretend your way into a new life. You have to grow into the person who truly lives it. This process is about more than just changing your actions; it's about shifting how you see yourself.

Start by getting curious. Imagine the version of you who already has what you want. How do they think, act, and show up in the world? What do they believe about themselves? This is about stepping into that energy and making it real. Embodying it. One choice at a time and one habit at a time.

My friend Alessia Citro (yes, the one who wrote the foreword to this book) is a habits expert. After her own experience with shedding layers of an identity so ingrained in corporate achievements, working in high-tech sales at companies like Salesforce and Google, she felt so passionate about why habits are foundational to everything we desire, she wrote a book about it.

In her book, *Higher Self Habits: The Scientific, Strategic, and Spiritual Framework to Get Out of Your Own Way—For Good*,[21] Alessia said, "Habits are the bridge between who you are and who you're meant to be."

She explains that when you consistently choose small intentional actions that reflect your higher self, you start to close the gap between who you are now and who you're meant to be. It's about making real, sustainable change—not through willpower or hustle, but by building habits that are rooted in self-love and aligned with your values. Alessia reinforces that habits aren't about perfection or rigid discipline. It's more about having a practical roadmap that includes daily rituals "or a menu of higher self options" that support your growth, your well-being, and your most authentic life.

I'm not quite sure where I first heard the phrase "the algorithm of the Holy Spirit," but I'm confident that algo brought Alessia, her work, friendship, and mentorship into my life because I had already been doing the work to align myself with the frequency that would bring a high-quality human (is this another domain I need to buy?) like her into my life—at a time I needed it most.

I'll share more about intentionally cultivating the high-value friendships that match your new energy and SMART goals in the next chapter, so let's keep moving on your identity transformation.

---

21 Alessia Citro, *Higher Self Habits: The Scientific, Strategic, and Spiritual Framework to Get Out of Your Own Way—For Good* (Scottsdale, AZ: inhabit LLC, 2024).

Building Habits Aligned with Your Highest Potential

Goals are destinations. Habits are the fuel. Without daily fuel, your shiny SMART goals are as good as the social reels and captions you created but are too in-your-head to actually publish due to the perfectionism and fear-of-being-seen shadows you're still working on. (I'm calling myself out—or rather, I'm calling myself UP—a fun term I learned this year.)

You must (we must!) design habits that prove your (our!) new identity *today*. Just like Alessia wrote *Higher Self Habits* because it was a book she desperately needed to get out of her own way, I'm writing this book because I know it's going to help you and me level up, baby. I'm calling you UP—not calling you OUT (OK, maybe just a little).

Why Habits Matter

Habits are the autopilot of your life. The right ones make success inevitable; the wrong ones make it impossible. Start small. Stack new habits onto existing routines. Celebrate every win, no matter how tiny. Remember: Consistency beats intensity.

How to Build Better Habits

- **Habit Stacking:** Pair a new habit with something automatic (e.g., gratitude or doing a wall sit to build leg strength while brushing your teeth).

- **Environment Design:** Make good habits obvious; hide the junk. Alessia talks about moving the less-than-healthy food to the top shelf of her pantry so she doesn't see it at eye level, and if she really wants it, she has to get a stool to reach it. Something I've done is shut off any social media or email notification on my phone. Honestly, the constant "ping" "ping" is so freaking distracting when you're trying to do deep work, and it stimulated my nervous system to where I felt like Pavlov's dogs, but instead of getting a treat when the bell rings on my phone, I get an influx of cortisol and anxiety. No, no more "pings," Do Not Disturb is highly leveraged, and Airplane Mode is used more in my home than when I forget to turn it on at the start of my flights. (I'm sorry, it's happened a few times. We survived. God Bless).

- **Accountability:** Text a friend "Done" each day. Miss two in a row? You owe them dinner at a VERY expensive restaurant of their choice—yes, their choice. You can see how problematic things can get if you're out of alignment, especially if they're vegan and you're obsessed with Akaushi Wagyu.

The point is, every day is a vote for the person you're becoming.

Are your daily actions aligned with your long-term vision, or are you sabotaging yourself with old patterns? Audit your calendar, your to-do list, and your energy. If the answer is no, don't beat yourself up. But you need to make adjustments quickly and course correct before you get so far off track it feels pointless to get back on the right track. (Spoiler: It's never too late as I'm sure you've gathered by now.)

You're building a life that works for you, not against you. Habits are your way to honor yourself and keep you accountable. Don't confuse them for punishment. Reframe *punishment* or *boring* to *empowerment* and *consistent*.

I love how this Neuro-Linguistic Programming (NLP) certification is just paying for itself.

Crafting Your New Personal Brand

Got the habits down? Noice. (We also used to say that in the early 2000s, pronounced like "Noooooooooiiiccceeee.") Now let's talk personal brand.

What Is a Personal Brand?

Stated simply, your personal brand is your reputation, both online and offline, but it's more than just how others see you. It's how you actually operate, even when no one is watching. Your true personal brand is built on consistency and integrity. Your personal brand comes to life through your everyday actions, choices, and values. Your personal brand is consistently reflected in how you live. What people see on your Instagram stories or the image you attempt to strategically curate is not the essence of your personal brand. It's way deeper than that.

It's how people perceive you, what they say about you when you're not in the room, and the impression you leave on the world. Your personal brand is the story you tell yourself and the world about who you are. Are you starting to see how this is so contextually relevant to our identity?

What if the way you see yourself is completely different from how others see you? This is why it's important to be clear and intentional about your personal brand. Decide how you want to be known. Think about the vibe you want to give off, the values you want to embody, and the strengths and traits you want people to associate with you.

Personal branding is the process of consciously shaping and managing that reputation. You identify your unique skills, experiences, and qualities, and then communicate them in a way that resonates with your target audience while staying true to yourself.

A strong personal brand can help you stand out from the crowd, attract opportunities, and build a loyal following. It can open doors to new career paths, speaking engagements, collaborations, and other exciting possibilities.

What's your new "elevator pitch" to yourself and others? The one that aligns with your higher self identity and habits? I won't dive into the full blueprint here, since my editor is keeping a close eye on my word count! If you want to explore this process in depth and go through the same step-by-step guidance I use with my coaching clients, you can learn more about how you can work with me in the Resources section at the end of the book.

If you search "personal branding" on Google, YouTube, and social, you'll get a plethora of resources (just be wary of the people positioning themselves as experts who clearly are not). I will give a shout-out to Rory and AJ Vaden of Brand Builders Group as true experts. When I was digging into trying to understand and craft my own personal brand, I binged their content, and it really helped me get clear on who I wanted to serve. The personal stories they shared of their own "business breakups" and leaning into their personal values as a north star for their decision-making resonated deeply with me during a time I really needed it. Another shout-out to the algorithm of the Holy Spirit.

But, before we move on to the next section and chapter, I will give you a little something, something value-add. Because I want to give you something tangible to reference so you can intentionally make decisions and choices that are either a Randy Jackson with "it's a no for me, dawg" or a Gabby Bernstein or a Human Design–sacral authority affirming "hell yes."

Told you I'm a recovering people pleaser! So, let's create your Personal Brand Guidelines doc!

Creating Your Personal Brand Guidelines

When a company undergoes a rebrand, one of the first steps is revisiting its original brand guidelines. If you're a marketer reading this, clearly, I don't have to explain this.

For anyone new here, brand guidelines serve as the foundation for a company's or brand's identity, outlining everything from its mission and values to its visual identity and tone of voice.

During a rebrand, the company refines and updates these guidelines to reflect the new brand attributes it wants to bring to life. Brand guidelines are more than just a document—they're a tool for ensuring consistency and alignment. Companies use them to make decisions about everything from marketing campaigns to partnerships, ensuring that every choice reflects the brand's identity.

Think of your personal brand as your own set of brand guidelines. Just like a company, you have a mission, values, and unique attributes that define who you are and what you stand for. And you can refine them any time you want to make a material change in your life so you can ensure your personal brand guidelines align with the elevated person you are now—or want to become.

Your personal brand guidelines can serve as a decision-making framework for your life, dawg. (I had to.)

What Goes into a Brand Guidelines Document?

- **Mission Statement:** Your why. It's your purpose, your reason for being, and the impact you want to make on the world.

- **Core Values:** The principles that guide your life. They reflect what's most important to you and serve as a compass for your decisions.

- **Brand Attributes:** The qualities that make you unique. They're the traits that define your personality and how you show up in the world.

- **Visual Identity:** How you present yourself to the world. It includes your personal style, your grooming, and even your online presence.

- **Tone of Voice:** How you communicate with others. It's the way you speak, write, and express yourself.

- **Usage Guidelines:** The boundaries and standards you set for yourself. They help you stay true to your values and ensure that your actions align with your personal brand.

Using Your Personal Brand Guidelines as a Decision-Making Framework

Once you've created your personal brand guidelines, you can use them as a tool for making aligned decisions in your life.

- **Career Decisions:** Does this job or project align with my mission, values, and goals?

- **Relationships:** Does this person support and respect my values?

- **Opportunities:** Does this opportunity reflect who I am and what I stand for?

- **Daily Choices:** Are my actions today consistent with my personal brand?

If the answer is yes, the decision is "in compliance" with your personal brand guidelines. If the answer is no, it's a sign that the decision might not be the right fit for you. (I was so tempted to, "dawg" you, but alas, I'm evolving—and, again, paying my editor by the word.)

Integrating Your New Identity in Everyday Life

Identity is who you are at your core, which includes the beliefs, values, and self-concept that guide you, even when no one is watching. Your personal brand reflects how that identity comes across to others and how people experience you. When your inner self and your outward presence match, you are living as your true self, both inside and out.

Begin to act as the person you want to become. Make choices that align with your new identity rather than your old limitations. Over time, these actions will reinforce your new story until it becomes second nature.

You are building more than just a new brand. You're becoming the person who lives and breathes this new way of being, inspiring others along the way. This transformation is about showing up as the real, radiant, rebranded you.

Identity transformation is the final piece of your rebrand. Seeing yourself in a new light leads to new actions and, ultimately, new results. This is how lasting change takes root.

CALL TO ACTION

Holy shit! We are getting so close to your total transformation. We're starting a new section next where we discuss building a network and community that supports your new identity, goals, and personal brand! So, before you move on, I have some exercises for you to complete so you can get really clear on the people and network aligned with your rebrand.

IF YOU HAVE **THE REBRAND YOU COMPANION WORKBOOK,** HEAD TO THE SECTION OF THE CORRESPONDING CHAPTER AND COMPLETE THE ASSOCIATED QUESTIONS AND PROMPTS.

Exercise: Meet Your Higher Self

- Close your eyes and fast-forward three years. Best-you walks in.

- What's their energy like? How do they speak, stand, decide?

- Jot the first words that pop: confident, playful, boundary-boss, whatever.

- Circle three traits that make you grin. Those are your identity anchors.

Exercise: Audit Your Current Routines

- Where are you spending your time and energy? What needs to change?

- Choose one new habit to build this week. Make it small, specific, and easy to track.

- Align your calendar with your goals. Schedule time for your most important actions—don't leave them to chance.

Exercise: Create Your Personal Brand Guidelines

1. Define Your Mission Statement: What is your purpose? What impact do you want to make on the world?
   Example: To inspire and empower others to live authentically and achieve their full potential.

2. Identify Your Core Values: Reflect on the values you identified earlier in this book.
   Example: Integrity, creativity, connection, growth, and service.

3. Clarify Your Brand Attributes: Think about the qualities that make you unique.
   Example: Authentic, empathetic, innovative, driven, and approachable.

4. Define Your Visual Identity: Consider how you want to present yourself to the world.
   Example: A polished, professional style with a touch of creativity and individuality.

5. Develop Your Tone of Voice: Reflect on how you want to communicate with others.
   Example: Warm, conversational, and motivational.

6. Set Your Usage Guidelines: Establish boundaries and standards for how you make decisions.
   Example: I will only pursue opportunities that align with my values and long-term goals.

All done? Sweet. In Chapter 16, we're going to start with why relationships are critical to this new high-vibe version of you and achieving those big ol' goals, baby!

STEP 6

R

E

B

R

A

Network and Build Your Community

D

CHAPTER 16

The Power of Relationships

Just as brands don't succeed in a vacuum, your personal rebrand needs a community to thrive. In marketing, building an audience and nurturing relationships is what turns a campaign into retention, referrals, and repeat revenue. The same is true for you: The people you connect with will become your advocates, collaborators, and the ones who open doors you never knew existed.

You were not put on this planet to go it alone. I don't care how independent, introverted, or "I got this" you are—life is a team sport. And if you're reading this thinking, *But I'm fine on my own,* I'm here to lovingly call you out. Because the truth is, relationships are the secret sauce to a fulfilling, successful, and meaningful life. And that's why intentionally connecting with aligned people will set you up for success with your rebrand.

We live in a culture that glorifies the self-made, the lone wolf, the "I did it all by myself" narrative. It's everywhere: in business, in movies, in those cringey LinkedIn posts. But here's the reality check: No one, and I mean no one, gets anywhere truly great alone. Even the most iconic "self-made" people had mentors, friends, partners, and communities behind the scenes.

Yes, I'm calling you out, but I'm also calling you UP. Because I was the poster child for the Lone Wolf Club, membership of one.

As an only child from a divorced family with the occasional every-other-weekend visitations with my biological father, I was largely raised by a single mom. Before I jump in, I want to be clear that I love both of my parents, and I know they both did the best they could at the time under the circumstances and information they had. We often forget that our parents have their own baggage, limiting beliefs, and trauma that impact how they operate in life. So, a little empathy can go a long way, in many (not all) cases. For my unique upbringing, I have zero grudges and believe everything happened the way it was meant to in order to build me into the person I am today.

One thing I learned early on is that if something was going to get done, it was up to me. I'll never forget what my mom told me right before I entered kindergarten. She pulled me aside and said, "Now, make sure you pay attention in class, Alexis, because Mommy can't help you with your homework." It wasn't because she worked late; it was because she was admitting she couldn't help intellectually. She made that clear, and I realized what that meant for me. I would have to figure out and navigate every rite-of-passage milestone on my own—filling out a W-9 for my first job, walking into a bank branch and asking the teller how to open an account so I could cash my first paycheck (because my mom didn't believe in checking accounts or trust banks back then), completing FAFSA forms for college, and filling out college applications.

That independence and self-sufficiency followed me into adulthood, as did the parentification, enmeshment, and role reversal. It served a purpose, but it also came with drawbacks that led to the formation of several limiting beliefs. For a long time, I believed I had to handle everything on my own. I wore my self-sufficiency like a badge of honor, mixed with a strong sense of "I don't need anyone" and constant alertness. This over-the-top self-reliance followed me through every big change, new job, and challenge well into my late thirties. I never wanted to ask anyone for help because I thought it made me look less competent. Weak. Always the helper, never the helpee. Always the giver, but rarely the receiver. The more I DIY'd every area of my life, the more burned out and resentful I became.

Can you relate to feeling like you're carrying the world on your shoulders—alone? If you're nodding your head up and down in agreement, I wish I could give you a huge hug. It's exhausting. Have you dug into why you feel unsupported, if it's not already clear for you? I had to dig deep to uncover this for myself.

Through intense introspection, I understand a lot of where this mindset came from, much of it rooted in early childhood programming and not wanting to be perceived with labels such as "taking advantage of someone," "gold digger," "manipulator," "selfish," "center of attention," "needy," and wanting to be perceived as the opposite.

Often, when we do come to the point of admitting we need help, the catalyst is something that forces us: like recovering from a surgery and needing your boyfriend to wash your hair or realizing you can't hide in your house anymore after an unexpected career event, even if you haven't quite figured out your next move, and need to crawl out from under your shame rock despite your identity feeling totally foreign—or absent.

Have you been hibernating for too long in hermit mode?

The thing we have to remind ourselves of is that life is so much better when you do it with other people—LIFE, not just sex (I mean, that's cool too, though). And guess what? After healing and then spinning my wheels trying to figure out "what's next," the moment I became intentional about building community, my life and career took off.

I don't want you to waste any more time thinking you have to do everything solo.

We're Wired for Connection

Science has a lot to say about why relationships matter. In fact, it's one of the most consistent findings in psychology, neuroscience, and even biology: Humans are social creatures. We're wired for connection.

One of the most famous studies on this is the Harvard Study of Adult Development, which has followed participants for over eighty years. The big takeaway? Good relationships keep us happier and healthier. Period. Not money. Not fame. Not six-pack abs. Relationships. I'm sure you've heard stories about rich people who on their death beds admit that none of that money mattered, that they were still unhappy because they didn't have anyone to share experiences with.

Robert Waldinger, the current director of the study, put it like this: "The clearest message that we get from this seventy-five-year study is this: Good relationships keep us happier and healthier. Period."[22] People who are more socially connected to family, friends, and community are happier, physically healthier, and live longer than people who are less well connected.

And it's not just about having a ton of friends or being the life of the party. It's about the quality of those relationships. People in satisfying relationships, even if they have a small circle, recover from setbacks faster, experience less stress, and even have better immune systems. (Yes, your best friend might actually be keeping you from getting the flu. #Science!)

---

22 Robert Waldinger and Marc Schulz, *The Good Life: Lessons from the World's Longest Scientific Study of Happiness* (New York: Simon & Schuster, 2023), 25.

The Loneliness Epidemic

Now, let's talk about the flip side. We're living in what some experts call a "loneliness epidemic." Despite being more "connected" than ever (thanks, social media), more people report feeling isolated, lonely, and unsupported. And loneliness isn't just a bummer—it's a health risk. Studies show that chronic loneliness can be as damaging to your health as smoking fifteen cigarettes a day.[23] It increases your risk of heart disease, depression, anxiety, and even early death.

Let that sink in. Being lonely is literally bad for your health. So if you're tempted to brush off relationships as "nice to have," think again. They're as essential as food, water, and sleep.

Relationships Are Your Greatest Asset

OK, so relationships are good for your health. But what about your career, your business, your dreams? Duh. Relationships are your greatest asset. They open doors, spark ideas, provide support, and help you grow in ways you can't even imagine.

And it's not just about networking (ugh, I hate that word). It's about genuine connection. People want to help people they like, trust, and feel connected to. That's human nature. When you invest in relationships, you're investing in your future.

We'll talk about strategies for finding new people to build relationships with in the next chapter as well as mastermind events, which is where I met relationship-building expert Jeff Fenster. Jeff is a serial entrepreneur, speaker, podcast host, and bestselling author of *Relation-*

---

[23] Julianne Holt-Lunstad et al., "Loneliness and Social Isolation as Risk Factors for Mortality: A Meta-Analytic Review," *Perspectives on Psychological Science* 10, no. 2 (2015): 227–237, https://doi.org/10.1177/1745691614568352.

ship Bank Account: How to Make Friends, Have Fun, and Attract Lifelong Success. The book features contributions from notable figures such as Drew Brees, Neil Patel, and Pat Flynn, among others.

Jeff credits his success, like previously being recognized as one of America's top one hundred entrepreneurs under thirty-five and finalist for CEO of the Year by Ernst & Young, to what he calls "Relationship Capital." His philosophy is that building strong relationships—with everyone from the cashier at the grocery store to a Fortune 500 CEO—is the foundation for long-term success in business and life.[24] In his book, he shares stories and practical advice about how everyone knows someone, which means your conversation with someone who looks nothing like your ideal prospect likely has a best friend, brother, or cousin who is your ideal prospect.

Think about the best opportunities you've ever had. The job you landed, the client who took a chance on you, the mentor who gave you that game-changing advice. I'd bet that almost all of them came through a relationship. Not a cold application. Not a random stroke of luck. A relationship.

With the exception of my very first job (because, let's be honest, I didn't know anyone yet), every single job I've ever gotten was through a referral. Every. Single. One. That's not a coincidence. That's the power of relationships in action.

Think of your relationships as your personal brand's audience. The more you invest in them, the more your rebrand will gain traction, credibility, and reach.

---

24 Jeff Fenster, *Relationship Bank Account: How to Make Friends, Have Fun, and Attract Lifelong Success* (Hoboken, NJ: Wiley, 2023).

The Ripple Effect: How Relationships Multiply Your Impact

Here's where it gets really good. Relationships don't just add value to your life—they multiply it. When you build strong connections, you create a ripple effect. Your ideas spread further. Your influence grows. Your support system expands. You become a magnet for opportunities, resources, and good vibes.

And think about this through a marketing lens. Brands are initially built around offering a product or service. But they grow by earning the trust of their audience and community, which leads to brand affinity, loyalty, and referrals. The same is true for you. You can have the best skills, the most impressive resume, or the coolest business idea—but if you don't have relationships, you're shouting into the void.

Think about your favorite brands. Why do you keep coming back? It's not just the product. It's the feeling of being seen, valued, and part of something bigger. That's what relationships do. They turn transactions into loyalty, acquaintances into advocates, and dreams into reality.

Evidence from the World of Work

Let's look at the workplace. Gallup's research on employee engagement[25] found that people who have a "best friend at work" are more likely to be engaged, productive, and loyal. They're less likely to leave, more likely to go above and beyond, and even have fewer accidents on the job. Why? Because relationships create trust, psychological safety, and a sense of belonging.

---

25 Alok Patel and Stephanie Plowman, "The Increasing Importance of a Best Friend at Work," Gallup, August 16, 2022, updated January 19, 2024, https://www.gallup.com/workplace/397058/increasing-importance-best-friend-work.aspx.

In entrepreneurship, the most successful founders are those who build strong networks. They find cofounders, advisers, investors, and customers through relationships. They don't just pitch—they connect. They listen. They collaborate. And when things get tough (because they always do), it's their relationships that help them weather the storm.

Relationship ROI

If you're still not convinced, let's talk about ROI—return on investment. Relationships are the ultimate life hack. They make you happier, healthier, more successful, and more resilient. They help you bounce back from failure, celebrate your wins, and find meaning in the everyday.

And here's the kicker: The more you invest in relationships, the more you get back. It's exponential. One introduction leads to another. One conversation sparks a new idea. One act of kindness creates a ripple that comes back to you in ways you can't predict.

Brands that focus only on transactions—making the sale, closing the deal—might win in the short term. But the brands that build relationships? They win for life. They create loyal fans, passionate advocates, and communities that stick around through thick and thin.

You are your own brand. If you want to rebrand your life, don't just focus on what you can do or what you can offer. Focus on who you can connect with, how you can serve, and the community you can build. That's where the magic happens.

If you take one thing from this chapter, let it be this: You are not alone, and you're not supposed to be. Relationships are the foundation of a life well-lived. They're the bridge between where you are and where you want to go. They're the safety net when you fall and the fuel for your ascent.

So, what does this mean for you? It means you need to invest in your relationships with your friends and family, with your professional network, and with your community. These are the people who will cheer you on, pick you up, and open doors you didn't even know existed. Oh, and don't forget to invest in the relationship with yourself.

CALL TO ACTION

IF YOU HAVE *THE REBRAND YOU COMPANION WORKBOOK,* HEAD TO THE SECTION OF THE CORRESPONDING CHAPTER AND COMPLETE THE ASSOCIATED QUESTIONS AND PROMPTS.

Who are the people in your life you want to invest in? How can you show up for them? And how can you start building new connections that align with your goals and values?

To get tactical, create a new document in your Rebrand You folder, and complete the following exercises:

- Make a list of the people you want to invest in.

- Who are your "inner circle"?

- Who are the acquaintances you'd like to get to know better?

- Reach out to someone you haven't spoken to in a while. Send a text, an email, or even a handwritten note.

- Schedule regular check-ins with your closest friends and mentors. Put it on your calendar.

- Look for opportunities to help others. Share a resource, make an introduction, or offer your support.

- Be present. When you're with someone, put away your phone and really listen.

Remember, relationships are essential. They form the foundation of everything good in life. Invest in them, nurture them, and watch your life transform. In the next chapter, we'll explore how to find your people!

CHAPTER 17

Finding Your People and Building Your Community

In marketing, brands engage their audience, nurture their community, and create spaces for connection. You need to do the same in your life.

And if you're thinking, *But, Alexis, making friends as an adult feels about as natural as Dolly Parton's boobs.* First off, that's what first came to mind for you when you thought of the opposite of natural. You're weird. But, also, yes.

I hear you. You want to find your people, but where are they? How do you go from "Hey, nice weather we're having" to "You're my ride or die, let's build empires together"?

If you've ever felt like you're on the outside looking in or you're craving deeper connections but don't know where to start, you're not alone. The good news? Building and growing your community is not only possible—it's one of the most rewarding things you'll ever do for your life, your career, and your soul.

All right, let's get tactical. You know relationships matter. Now let's talk about how to actually find your people and keep those connections strong.

Vibe Check

As adults, our circles can shrink. We move, we change jobs, we outgrow old friendships, or we just get busy. But don't worry 'bout a thing. Because you can always find new people, new energy, and new opportunities for connection—IF, and I mean if, you're willing to put yourself out there. If the thought of going to an event solo terrifies you, it's understandable. But I'm living proof that it can be done, and many times, it's even better than going with someone else because you don't have a "crutch," and it allows you to float around like a butterfly without making sure the person you showed up with is attached to your hip at the same time.

When I first moved to Scottsdale, Arizona, after selling my house, ending an engagement, and traveling across the country with just myself and my two pups, it took me about six months of "I just made the worst mistake blowing up my entire life and moving here" before I had the guts to accept a casual invite to attend a "party in a park." A guy who I had met sitting at a restaurant bar solo during my business travels was not only a pharmaceutical sales rep, he was also passionate about house music and was a DJ on the weekends. He was going to be DJ'ing at an afternoon event in a park in Scottsdale and said I should stop by. I didn't really even know what house music was, technically. I mean I listen to music in my *house* all the time, which typically consists of Misfits, Bad Religion, Authority Zero, Pennywise and Face to Face—with the occasional country, Britney, reggae, and whatever other mood I'm in sprinkled into the mix. Yes, still a punk rock princess since my middle school days.

"But I don't know anyone, and he's going to be DJ'ing the whole time, so it's not like I can talk to him, and I can't be a weirdo and stand by the DJ stand the whole time. I shouldn't go. I should definitely go. No. Ugh, OK, I'll just go for like thirty minutes. Oh, and I'll bring my dogs, so they can be my friends."

Well, I ended up stepping outside of my comfort zone. I brought a blanket to sit on with my dogs, and as it were, conversations just organically happened. It didn't hurt that my dogs were adorable. (Dogs are great conversation starters—if you're single or looking to make friends and you want one and can responsibility take care of one, get you a dog! They get you out of your house, and assuming your dog is friendly and cute—I mean they're all cute—people will just come up to you because your dog is way cooler than you.)

To make a long story short, I ended up making several new friends that day, some of whom I still keep in touch with eleven years later.

But, yes, compared to when we were kids, building adult friendships is a bit trickier. And, as Mel Robbins talked about in her book, *The Let Them Theory*,[26] there are three things that matter most with adult relationships: energy, proximity, and timing.

Energy is everything. You know that feeling when you meet someone and you just click—like you've known them your whole life? Or, on the flip side, when you leave a conversation feeling like you need a nap and a sage smudge? Sure, someone could've been having a bad day, but pay attention to the vibes and your gut instinct when meeting new people. The right people will energize you, inspire you, and make you feel more like yourself—not less.

Proximity matters too. Yes, you can build amazing relationships online (more on that in a minute), but there's something powerful about being in the same room, sharing space, and having those spontaneous "let's grab coffee" moments. Sometimes, just showing up is half the battle.

Timing is the wild card. Sometimes you meet the right person at the wrong time, or you're not ready for a new connection until you've done some inner work. Be patient with yourself and others. The uni-

---

26 Mel Robbins and Sawyer Robbins, *The Let Them Theory: A Life-Changing Tool That Millions of People Can't Stop Talking About* (Carlsbad, CA: Hay House, 2024).

verse has a way of bringing the right people into your life when you're open and ready.

How to Find Your People

Let's get into the good stuff. Here are some practical, real-world ways to find your people—online, offline, and everywhere in between:

Follow Your Curiosity

The best way to meet new people is to do things that genuinely interest you—even if (especially if) they scare you a little. For me, post-corporate life began with improv comedy. I signed up for a class, not because I thought I'd be the next Nikki Glaser, but because I wanted to stretch myself, laugh, and meet people outside my usual circles. I was nervous. But I showed up, and I found a room full of people who were also willing to look ridiculous and try something new.

That led to a stand-up comedy class, which was even scarier (hello, spotlight and vulnerability!), but also wildly rewarding. And I was good at it—and am now paid to perform stand-up comedy! Comedy helped me own my story, find humor in the hard stuff, and connect with people through laughter.

The Power of Being in the Room and Events

There is so much truth to the saying "The Power of Being in the Room." This is all about visibility. This is why there are studies now about how much more difficult it is for younger generations and remote workers to gain access to the same opportunities as generations before them. Because it's undeniable that in-person experiences make it way easier and faster to build relationships and true connections with people. Online is better than nothing, but any time you have the chance to physically be in the same room as another person, take it. Decisions are made by the people who show up. Whether it's at the office, a networking event, a mastermind, or a book club, being in the room gives you access to opportunities, insights, and connections you can't get anywhere else.

After comedy, I started saying yes to more events that aligned with my interests and values. I went to an entrepreneur event through my alma mater, and there I met a woman who, like me, had a Pittsburgh connection. She'd left corporate to become a life coach. We clicked instantly, and our conversation reminded me that reinvention is possible at any stage in life.

I live in the Phoenix area, and I'm so grateful for how many options we have to find organizations that align with our interests and values. Groups like Powerhouse Women, Foundress, KNOW Women, Collab Culture, Hello Culture, and many others who cultivate community for women who are both entrepreneurs and working in corporate careers. There are also co-ed groups like The Table, and groups geared toward men. The goal is simply to be in community with like-minded people who aspire to achieve their potential and do good in the community we all live, work, and play.

Leverage Online Communities

Don't sleep on the power of online communities. I found Alessia online and joined her book club, which was a game-changer. Suddenly, I was surrounded (virtually) by smart, ambitious women who wanted to grow, learn, and support each other. That book club "connection" led to me stepping outside of my comfort zone and applying to speak at an event called Speaker Spotlight, where I got to share my story and connect with even more like-minded people.

Coffee Dates and One-on-Ones

Big events are great, but real connection often happens in smaller settings. I started reaching out to people I met—at events, online, wherever—and inviting them for coffee (virtually or in-person). Sometimes it was a quick chat; sometimes it turned into a two-hour deep dive into life, business, and everything in between. The point is, don't be afraid to take things offline and make it personal. This is where you get a chance to see if the person you met at the event is the same brand of "weird" you are, share similar values, and can swap funny stories from high school, college and laugh about how different life is compared to our awkward pasts.

The connection can go even deeper—like pulling in your significant others for a double date—and then the significant others realizing they're the same brand of weird, and now suddenly they're golfing together the next weekend—without you two. The point is, cool connections can happen when you're in a more intimate get-to-know-you setting. It's not something to be forced, there's no promises guaranteed, no hard feelings if there's not a friendship spark and you don't want to take it beyond pleasant-acquaintance status, but when there's a spark, it's so damn cool making a new, genuine adult friend!

Offline/ IRL/In-Person Ideas

- Classes and workshops (improv, cooking, art, fitness—whatever lights you up)

- Local networking events (check your alma mater, professional associations, or Meetup.com)

- Conferences and retreats (look for ones that align with your interests or industry)

- Volunteering (find a cause you care about and show up)

- Community groups (book clubs, hiking groups, faith communities, etc.)

- Other public spots (coffee shops, coworking spaces, or even your local dog park)

IRL Pro Tips

- Compliment people everywhere you go. People love to feel seen

- Be curious. Ask what someone's reading, what they ordered, what lights them up

- Smile and say hi to everyone. Being warm and approachable is a skill, and it opens doors

- Don't expect anything in return. The energy you put out always comes back, even if it's not from the same person

Online Ideas

- Group coaching or membership community for business or lifestyle interests

- Facebook groups and online forums (search for your interests + "community")

- LinkedIn groups and virtual networking events

- Book clubs or online mastermind groups

- Instagram, TikTok, Threads, X, etc. (don't be afraid to DM someone you admire)

- Online courses and workshops (many have built-in communities)

- Slack or Discord groups for your industry or hobbies

The key is to show up, participate, and be open to connection. You don't have to be the loudest or most outgoing person in the room (or the Zoom). Just be curious, be kind, and be yourself. If you'd told me a few years ago that I'd be building a business and a community at the same time, I would have laughed (nervously). For so long, I thought I had to do it all myself. But the moment I started leaning into community, everything changed.

Improv and stand-up taught me to embrace uncertainty and connect through vulnerability. Entrepreneur events introduced me to people who "got it"—the highs, the lows, the "what the hell am I doing?" moments. Book clubs and masterminds gave me a space to learn, share, and grow with others on a similar path. Coffee dates turned acquaintances into friends, and retreats turned friends into family.

Every time I said yes to a new experience, I found another piece of my community puzzle. Sometimes it was a deep connection, sometimes just a fun conversation, but every interaction mattered. And the more I leaned in, the more opportunities, support, and joy I found.

How are you finding or connecting with your people today? Are there groups in your community you're part of or want to be? If you live in an area where the closest thing to "your people" is your neighbor's rooster who says hello to you every morning at six, are you part of any online communities? A simple keyword search on Google or your favorite new AI tool can turn up cool online communities that I'm sure would be delighted to have you as a member!

How to Nurture Your People

Finding your people is just the start. Now you have to keep those relationships alive.

- **Add Value:** How can you help this person? Share a resource, offer advice, make an introduction.

- **Stay Connected:** Life gets busy, but a quick text or call goes a long way. Don't wait for a "reason" to reach out.

- **Remember the Little Things:** Birthdays, favorite coffee orders, the name of their dog—these details matter.

- **Be Consistent:** Relationships thrive on consistency. Make it a habit to check in.

- **Leverage Technology:** Use reminders, notes apps, calendars, AI, or even a CRM for your life. Take notes when you're meeting people, set a reminder for their birthday so you can send a message or call, and when you know you're going to see them again, pull that note up to help you remember key details and prep yourself with talking points for your meeting. This might sound a bit robotic, but as you get older, the ol' ticker can use an assist from time to time. So, notes are my BFF.

And the key thing for you to keep in mind is don't make relationships transactional. No one wants to feel like a means to an end. Be present, be curious, and be honest. People can sense desperation from a mile away. Don't be that person.

Recapping Energy, Proximity, and Timing

Let's circle back to those three keys.

Energy: Trust your gut. If someone lights you up, follow that spark. If you leave an event feeling drained, it's OK to move on. You're not for everyone, and not everyone is for you.

Proximity: Make it easy to connect. Choose events and groups that are convenient, or create your own meetups if you don't see what you want. Sometimes, just being in the right place at the right time is all it takes.

Timing: Be patient. Not every connection will turn into a lifelong friendship, and that's OK. You've heard the saying, some people are meant for a season, some for a reason, and some for a lifetime. It's so true. Stay open, and trust that your people are out there.

Your Community Is Waiting

Whether you're reinventing your career, starting a business, or just looking for more meaning and connection, your community is out there. Sometimes you find them in the most unexpected places—a comedy class, a coffee shop, a virtual book club, or a mastermind retreat. You don't have to do life alone.

Be brave enough to show up. Be open enough to say yes. And be patient enough to let the right people find you too.

Because when you find your people, everything gets easier, richer, and a whole lot more fun. And if you ever feel awkward or out of place, just remember that everyone else is probably feeling the same way. So go ahead—make the first move. Your future friends (and collaborators and cheerleaders and referrals) are waiting.

CALL TO ACTION

IF YOU HAVE THE REBRAND YOU COMPANION WORKBOOK, HEAD TO THE SECTION OF THE CORRESPONDING CHAPTER AND COMPLETE THE ASSOCIATED QUESTIONS AND PROMPTS.

Who can you reconnect with this week? What events or groups can you join to meet new people? How can you add value to your community? Start small, be consistent, and watch your network—and your life—transform.

Here are some practical exercises to kickstart your community-building mission:

1. Audit the Energy

- **Reflect:** Think about the people you spend the most time with. Who energizes you? Who drains you? Write down a list of both.

- **Analyze:** What patterns do you notice? Are there certain types of people or situations that consistently lift you up or bring you down?

- **Adjust:** Make a conscious effort to spend more time with the people who energize you and less time with the ones who drain you. This might mean setting boundaries, saying no to certain invitations, or seeking out new connections.

2. Get Curious

- **Brainstorm:** What are you curious about? What have you always wanted to try? Make a list of at least five things that spark your interest, no matter how big or small.

- **Research:** Look for classes, workshops, events, or groups related to your interests. Check local community centers, online forums, or Meetup.com.

- **Commit:** Choose one activity from your list and sign up for it. It could be a one-time workshop, a weekly class, or a virtual meetup. The point is to take action and put yourself out there.

3. Connect and Reconnect

- **Identify:** Think of three people you admire, want to reconnect with, or simply want to get to know better. They could be people you've met at events, online, or through mutual connections.

- **Personalize:** Craft a genuine message to each person. Don't just send a generic "Let's connect!" message. Mention something specific that you admire about them, a shared interest, or a topic you'd like to discuss.

- **Invite:** Invite them for a virtual coffee, a quick call, or a casual meetup. Make it easy for them to say yes by suggesting a specific time and place.

- **Ask and Listen:** Once you connect, remember this golden rule: People love to talk about themselves! If you're feeling a little nervous, shift the focus by asking open-ended questions about *them*. This takes the pressure off you and genuinely shows your curiosity. Think about questions like "What's been the most exciting project you've worked on recently?" or "What's a challenge you're currently enjoying tackling?" Then, truly listen to their answers.

4. The Online Community Dive

- **Search:** Use keywords related to your interests, industry, or goals to find online communities on Facebook, LinkedIn, Slack, Discord, or other platforms.

- **Join:** Join at least three communities that seem like a good fit.

- **Engage:** Don't just lurk! Introduce yourself, ask questions, share your insights, and participate in discussions. Be a valuable member of the community, not just a passive observer.

5. Experiment IRL

- **Explore:** Identify a local coffee shop, coworking space, community center, or other gathering place that aligns with your interests or values.

- **Visit:** Make a point to visit that place at least once a week.

- **Connect:** Strike up conversations with people you meet there. Ask about their work, their hobbies, or their day. Be curious and open to connection.

6. Be Seen (and Vulnerable)

- **Share:** On social or in one of your online or offline communities, share something vulnerable about yourself. It could be a challenge you're facing, a fear you're working to overcome, or a dream you're pursuing.

- **Receive:** Allow yourself to be seen and supported by others. Resist the urge to downplay your vulnerability or apologize for sharing.

- **Reflect:** How did it feel to be vulnerable? What did you learn from the experience? How did it impact your connection with others?

As you rebrand your life, don't just focus on your resume, your skills, or your goals. Focus on your relationships. Invest in them. Nurture them. Celebrate them. Because at the end of the day, it's not what you have or what you do—it's who you do it with that matters most.

It's all about a mindset of growing with your community, and speaking of a growth mindset, we're headed into the final section of the REBRAND Framework, Develop a Growth Mindset, next.

STEP 7

R
E
B
R
A
N

Develop a Growth Mindset

CHAPTER 18

Test and Learn

So, you've set your goals, mapped your action plan, launched your new campaign concept, and you're beginning to live that rebrand life. Congrats on phase one. Now, we need to talk about phase two—when the data starts rolling in and the feedback gets real.

We marketers call this the "test and learn" phase. This is where you get to see what's working, what's not, and what needs a little (or a lot) of tweaking. The best brands don't just launch and hope for success. They measure, optimize, and iterate. They expect to learn. And so should you.

No one gets it right the first time. Not in life, not in business, and definitely not in marketing. That's why marketers are always experimenting. We test different headlines, images, calls to action, and even the tiniest details like CTA button colors. Then we analyze what works, what doesn't; we tweak (or twerk—if it's working), optimize, and test again.

Your life is no different. Think of it as being in R & D mode, a constant state of testing and learning. The actions you take, the habits you build, and the decisions you make are all part of an ongoing experiment. Some things will work, and others won't—and that's OK. The goal isn't perfection; it's progress. It's about learning from every experience, making adjustments, and moving forward.

In this chapter, we're going to talk about how to adopt a test-and-learn mindset in your life. You'll learn how to treat your goals and actions like a marketing campaign, create a testing plan, embrace setbacks as opportunities to grow, and celebrate the wins.

A reminder to my fellow perfectionists: It's not about getting it perfect. It's about getting curious. It's about treating your life like the world's most important marketing campaign—because it is.

The Test-and-Learn Mindset

Marketers live by the test-and-learn approach. Every test, whether it succeeds or flops, provides valuable insights.

You can apply this same mindset to your life. We'll get into specifics shortly, but here's the high-level on what to drill into your brain (ITOE)—thank me later when it works, and I'm like "I toe you so." (Couldn't help myself.)

- **Iterate:** Evaluate your goals, actions, and habits regularly. What's working? What's not?

- **Test:** Readjust your goals. Try new approaches, habits, or strategies to see what works best.

- **Optimize:** Use the insights from your tests to make adjustments and improve your results.

- **Embrace Failure:** View setbacks as opportunities to learn and grow. It's just data.

The beauty of this mindset is that it takes the pressure off. You don't have to have it all figured out. You just have to be willing to experiment, learn, pivot, or stay the course—just keep going.

How Marketers Do It (and How You Can, Too)

Here's another call UP to my hypercritical perfectionist pals. Let's be real. When many of us set goals, try something new, and then when it doesn't go perfectly, we tend to spiral. Cue the *I suck at this, Why did I even try?* and *Maybe I'm just not cut out for this* brain chatter.

But when we do more nervous system healing and mindset work, we start to realize that's not how growth works. It's hard when you have a gold-star, mastery mentality and then not have it work right away. But guess what? That's not how marketing works, and it's definitely not how *rebranding* you works.

So, if you try something new and you're not an expert after thirty days, chill. Give yourself some grace. Take a lap. Walk the dog. Drink some water. Because the test-and-learn mindset is about curiosity, not judgment. It's about collecting data. Every result is feedback, not a verdict. You're not failing—you're learning. You're not stuck—you're iterating.

And I'll prove it to you. Let's take a look at my personal SMART goals I shared with you back in Chapter 13.

My Own "Test and Learn" Journey

After a campaign launches, marketers check the numbers, read the comments and media coverage, and ask, "What's resonating? What's falling flat? Where are we seeing unexpected results?"

You get to do the same thing with your life. You set your SMART goals, you take action, and then you *check in*. What's working? What's not? Where are you feeling resistance or excitement? What needs a tweak?

I'm not just preaching this—I'm living it. Here's how I'm testing, learning, and optimizing my own SMART goals. First, let me give you the format:

Goal:
What are you working toward?

What I Tried:
What actions did you take? What did you launch, change, or experiment with?

What Worked:
What went well? What results or positive feedback did you notice?

What Didn't:
What didn't go as planned? Where did you feel resistance, frustration, or lack of results?

What I'm Tweaking:
What immediate adjustment or pivot are you making based on what you learned?

Next Experiment:
What new action, strategy, or idea will you try next? What's your next "test"?

Notes/Insights:
Any extra thoughts, patterns, or aha! moments you want to remember? Here is what it's looked like for me this year:

Goal 1:
Continue Marketing Consulting Client Work

What I Tried:
Reduced the number of clients I work with at a time, so I have time and capacity to work on my other goals.

What Worked:
Declined new clients and consulting engagements (scary as hell!). Leaned into trust, faith, and challenged my limiting belief around scarcity.

What Didn't:
Worked more than my stated hours because I love my existing clients, can't turn off my marketing strategy brain, and love to provide value. Overstepped my own boundaries and reduced the amount of time I had for other goals.

What I'm Tweaking:
Sticking to my retainer hours. Reminding myself I'm "not a corporate salaried employee" and therefore I can't constantly think about growing my clients' business more than my own.

Next Experiment:
Blocking off two days a week where clients know I'm not available. That will force me to better manage my time, not shift between projects in the same day, and I can be more efficient and creative.

Notes/Insights:
Remember, you are a consultant and not an employee. Your hours are billable and set. Anything over and above your hours requires a new scope of work and compensation for your time.

Goal 2:
Establish a Strong Brand and Online Presence

What I Tried:
Launched my website, started posting on Instagram, tried TikTok, and revived my LinkedIn. Invested in a monthly photo subscription service for headshots, lifestyle shots, B-roll, etc.

What Worked:
Beautiful new website live, new messaging on website.

What Didn't:
TikTok felt overwhelming. I'm not consistently posting on Instagram. Heavy comedy focus—posting about upcoming shows. Some people thinking I'm "just a comedian" now. I created content, but didn't post most of it due to overthinking and perfectionist tendencies.

What I'm Tweaking:
Messaging. Focusing on Instagram and LinkedIn. Scheduling content creation time. Using the content from the monthly photo service before I invest in new photography and asset development.

Next Experiment:
Get clear on my brand messaging and develop complementary content so people understand what my offers are and what I've been building post-corporate. Consider outsourcing some elements of social media management and content creation.

Notes/Insights:
Diversify content and stick to a consistent posting schedule.

Goal 3:
Launch and Monetize My Expertise

What I Tried:
Started 1:1 career, mindset, and life design coaching and created free lead magnet.

What Worked:
First coaching clients came from my network. Amazing testimonials!

What Didn't:
I didn't promote or advertise my coaching (I wasn't ready to yet), didn't promote the lead magnet.

What I'm Tweaking:
Begin proactively promoting coaching services to my network after book launch. Use free lead magnet to build email list.

Next Experiment:
Create an online course and workshop from the 1:1 coaching framework and book. Pursue corporate clients for consulting, workshops, and keynotes.

Notes/Insights:
Tout strong testimonials and start actively promoting offers across channels.

Goal 4:
Establish Myself as a Thought Leader

What I Tried:
Spoke at events, created a new signature talk, pitched for podcasts and conferences, and invested in a writers' retreat in Sedona to begin the book writing/publishing process.

What Worked:
Validation on new signature talk topic, attended writers' retreat and editor confirmed viability of book theme, landed podcast spots, conducted workshops, shared my stories vulnerably, and authentically built valuable relationships and connections.

What Didn't:
Rejection from some conference pitches (because I didn't have a book!). Miscalculated the amount of time finishing my book would take. Not following up with people who expressed interest during events I spoke at. Time management and bandwidth.

What I'm Tweaking:
Hired an editor and book coach to help me publish my book, being more selective about opportunities I say yes to, or pitch to—confirm alignment with long-term strategy and audience.

Next Experiment:
Consider starting my own podcast to facilitate long-form conversations around the topics I'm passionate about. Create and activate content strategy for promoting book and speaker services.

Notes/Insights:
Invest more time and energy on aligned opportunities and long-term goals. Identify support network.

Goal 5: Invest in Health, Relationships, Continuing Education, and Fun

What I Tried:
Took improv and stand-up classes, meal prepped, blocked mornings for workouts. Joined a mastermind, book club, womens' networking group, bought tickets for conferences, read lots of books.

What Worked:
Improv and stand-up classes led to paid comedy gigs and a new signature talk about conscious comedy, met new people through different groups, and consumed some great books.

What Didn't:
Overcommitted to events and comedy shows, fell out of my workout routine, got "too busy" to eat lunch many days, didn't hit my protein intake goals, didn't have much time for fun, not nurturing relationships with family and friends due to exhaustion and bandwidth.

What I'm Tweaking:
Focusing on daytime speaking/comedy opportunities and prioritizing quality time with loved ones. Getting back into my workout routine and setting a timer that forces me to eat lunch.

Next Experiment:
Have more fun. Intentionally schedule one new activity that brings joy and see how it impacts my energy and creativity. Hire personal trainer for more accountability.

Notes/Insights:
Love the hustle and journey of building a business, but don't lose sight of your health and relationships because without those, this business stuff doesn't even matter.

How Often to Conduct a "Test and Learn" Audit

So, how often should you be doing this? It depends. How much time ya got? You can do it daily, weekly, monthly, or quarterly. I'd definitely recommend doing it more often than annually. But if annually is all you got, then do that.

Something I've been doing for a few years now is staying at home on New Year's Eve and doing an end-of-year reflection and then setting intentions and new goals for the next year. A lot of people also like to pick a "word of the year" for the new year that represents the feeling or thing they want to "call in" for the year ahead. To give you an example of what your word of the year could be, my word for 2025 was *expansion*.

Time-bound, "Test and Learn" Ideas to Get You Started

- **Weekly Check-In:** Set aside ten minutes each week to review your goals and actions. Ask: What worked? What didn't? What surprised me?

- **Progress Journal:** Keep a running log of your experiments, pivots, and lessons learned. Celebrate the wins and get curious about the "flops."

- **Mini-Retrospective:** Once a month, do a deeper dive. What patterns are emerging? Where are you consistently thriving or struggling? What's one thing you'll try differently next month?

- **Feedback Loop:** Ask for feedback from trusted friends, mentors, or even your audience. Sometimes the best insights come from outside your own head.

Embrace the Process

The truth is, you're never "done." The best brands are always optimizing, always learning, always growing. The same goes for you. Your goals, your habits, your identity—they're all living, breathing things. You get to update them as you learn more about yourself and what lights you up.

So, don't be afraid to pivot. Don't be afraid to say, "Hey, this isn't working for me," and try something new. That's not failure—that's wisdom. That's growth. That's how you become the most authentic, high-vibe, rebranded version of you.

Remember: You're not a finished product. You're a living, breathing, ever-evolving brand. And the world needs that version of you.

CALL TO ACTION

IF YOU HAVE **THE REBRAND YOU COMPANION WORKBOOK,** HEAD TO THE SECTION OF THE CORRESPONDING CHAPTER AND COMPLETE THE ASSOCIATED QUESTIONS AND PROMPTS.

Ready to run your own test-and-learn cycle? It's time to optimize your life like a high-vibe, goal-getting boss! Here's how to use the Test-and-Learn Goal Tracker with your SMART goals and action steps:

1. Pick a SMART Goal:
Choose one of your specific, measurable, achievable, relevant, and time-bound goals from your action plan.

2. Take Action (Launch Your Campaign):
Put your action steps into play. This is your "go live" moment—send the email, post the content, sign up for the class, or start the new habit. Don't wait for perfect. Just launch.

3. Reflect (Check the Data):
What did you actually do? What worked? What didn't? Where did you feel momentum, and where did you hit a wall? Be honest—this is your campaign report, not a highlight reel.

4. Tweak (Optimize Your Strategy):
Based on what you learned, make a small adjustment. Maybe you need to change your approach, shift your schedule, or ask for help. This isn't failure—it's optimization, just like marketers do after a campaign launch.

5. Experiment Again (Test a New Angle):
Write down your next experiment. What's the next action, tweak, or bold move you'll try? Maybe it's a new time of day, a different platform, or a fresh accountability partner. Keep testing!

6. Repeat (Iterate Like a Pro):
Growth isn't a one-and-done. Use a new worksheet, page, section, etc. for each SMART goal, or revisit the same one as you keep refining. Every cycle brings you closer to your ideal life—and your highest self.

Pro Tip: Celebrate every insight, even the "well, that was a dumpster fire" moments. This is how you build confidence, resilience, and a life that's actually aligned with your values and vision. In Chapter 19, we're going to talk about why you need to embrace those insights and "tests"; it's all about embracing lifelong learning—because that's how we grow.

CHAPTER 19

Embrace Lifelong Learning, Change, and Growth

In marketing, the brands that get left behind are the ones who stop listening, stop testing, and stop growing. The same goes for your personal journey. Just like the most successful brands, your rebrand depends on your willingness to keep learning and adapting. Otherwise, you could end up like Blockbuster. Stay curious, and you'll always find new ways to refresh your brand as your personal and professional life changes with the times.

I once heard Robin Sharma, bestselling author of *The Monk Who Sold His Ferrari* book series, say on a podcast that every billionaire and creative genius he has interviewed shares one universal trait: unrelenting curiosity. They never stop asking questions. They don't take things at face value. They refuse to claim "expert" status. They're always learning, always growing, always wondering, *What else is possible?*

That hit so deep.

One of the things I always say to my friends—often after defending a crazy conspiracy theory meme I just texted them (which BTW is it REALLY a conspiracy or do we just need to wait six months before it hits the airwaves?), but, all joking aside, one of the things I always say is "I believe everything—and nothing—all at the same time."

What I mean by this is I'm always open to new information. Information that could completely obliterate or challenge what I thought was "true" or "right" or "how things work." I think it's so important for us to always be curious and open to new findings, new ways of doing things, and the potential for something new to challenge our existing beliefs.

I mean, look at how things have progressed over the last few decades. Remember as a kid watching *The Jetsons* cartoon (you Old Millennials and Gen Xers get it) and seeing George talk to his boss in a video chat on a big screen? "Woah, that could never happen in our lifetime!"

And look at you now taking every damn meeting over Zoom and Teams and FaceTiming your best friend who moved to the other side of the country for a job, who you can set a seat for at your Sunday brunch and make it like she's still in-person with the gang. (Warning: If I ever see you talking on FaceTime or speakerphone without headphones on in public, I will be so so so disappointed in you. Literally one of my biggest pet peeves, so keep this idea for being in the comfort of your own hosted-at-home brunch. K thanks.)

You can also think of cultural or political beliefs you had, that once you learned new information, made you reconsider your stance. The point is, it's wonderful to have an open mind and be willing to take in new information and new experiences that allow your perspective to evolve. Don't you think the world needs more of that independent, open thinking? I sure as hell do.

We should never be afraid, or prevented from, asking questions. About ANYTHING. I mean, isn't that what the scientific method is all about? Isn't that what design thinking is all about? Isn't that what marketing is all about?

As a self-proclaimed lifelong learner, the more I reflected on Robin Sharma's words, the clearer it became that curiosity is a superpower.

And you know what? That's not just a billionaire thing. That's a *human* thing. It's a you thing. If you're reading this, I bet you're naturally curious too. Maybe you're just starting to rediscover that spark of curiosity you had as a kid. Maybe you've always been the one asking "why?" Maybe you're the person who can't help but google random questions (like how long is a hummingbird's tongue) or has an intimate ethereal conversation with ChatGPT at 2 a.m. about whether or not you're a Pleiadian starseed who came to Earth to be a lightworker to help shepherd humanity into 5D consciousness (come on, I can't be the only one, I see you!).

Interdimensional beings and hummingbirds aside, curiosity is the foundation of a growth mindset. It's what keeps you moving forward when the world around you is changing faster than TikTok trends.

Seriously, by the time this book is published, there could very well be a development in AI that puts all my ChatGPT references in the obsolete bucket. But that's OK (and my editor would probably love making a few more buckets updating the book later on). It's OK because if we have a growth mindset, we know that the point of all of this is to learn, adapt, celebrate, and do it all over again—forever, like universal forever, according to my Pleiadian brothers and sisters. *Winks at you and makes Leonardo DiCaprio meme face*

You don't just "arrive" at growth, check it off your to-do list, and call it a day. If you're reading this, you already know that. The most successful people and brands on the planet? They know this. They're not just chasing the next big thing—they're committed to learning, adapting, and celebrating every step of the journey. They're curious. They're resilient. And they know how to throw a damn good celebration when they hit a milestone (and even when they don't).

Speaking of celebrating milestones, how about let's stop with the office pizza party celebrations and test out the direct-deposit-into-my-bank-account party theme. Stay curious, and test and learn, Corporate America, am I right? You may just uncover that employees smile even bigger when they have the agency and funds to purchase what they really want, which may not be a double-stuffed extra-large pepperoni pizza that makes them sleepy and unproductive after they walk back to their desk from the conference room and want to take a nap on their keyboard.

OK, I'll get off my soapbox now. You don't just rebrand once and call it a day. You keep iterating, learning, and celebrating every step. This chapter is your permission slip—and your roadmap—to keep growing, no matter what life throws your way. We're going to talk about how to stay curious, how to navigate change with grace, and how to celebrate your wins (big and small) so you stay inspired for the long haul.

Lifelong Learning Matters Now More Than Ever

If you want to stay ahead, you need to keep learning. Lifelong learning isn't just about picking up new skills (though, yes, that's awesome). It's about staying adaptable, relevant, and inspired. It's about keeping your mind sharp, your perspective fresh, and your confidence high. It's about waking up every day with the mindset that there's always something new to discover, something new to try, and something new to become—because there certainly is.

Here's why lifelong learning matters:

- **It Adapts to Constant Change:** Think about how quickly social media platforms like TikTok have changed the way brands (and people) market themselves (I'm still struggling with TikTok). Or how people are now turning more to ChatGPT to search for "best restaurant near me," and Google is now displaying generative AI summaries at the top of search results. Marketers now need a new strategy that prioritizes authority, structure, and clarity so their content gets cited, surfaced, and summarized where customers see it. In other words, the playbook is changing. The point is, staying curious lets you adapt to constant shifts in technology, culture, and science instead of getting left behind.

- **It Fuels Personal Growth:** Learning keeps you sharp. It's not just about knowledge—it's about becoming the best version of yourself.

- **It Opens Doors:** The more you learn, the more opportunities you create. New jobs, passion projects, meaningful connections—they all start with curiosity.

- **It Keeps You Resilient:** When you're committed to learning, you see setbacks as opportunities to grow, not reasons to give up.

Honestly, if I could be paid to be a professional student, I would take that all day long. I absolutely love studying new things, going down rabbit holes, or even just looking at the opposite sides of the argument of something I believe in. Taking an improv comedy class led me to take a stand-up writing class, which led me to a stand-up performance class, which led me to being a paid comedian. My curiosity about psychology and understanding human behavior, mindset, and neuroscience led me to research NLP and then take a course to become a certified NLP practitioner. And then to taking a Master Level NLP practitioner course, as well as getting certified in Mental Emotional Release® (MER) and Hypnotherapy. The next thing I want to learn is how to become an even better public speaker. So, I hired a speaking coach, and I'm considering joining Toastmasters or a similar formal speaker training program or organization.

Curiosity is like a muscle—the more you use it, the stronger it gets. When you stay curious, you're not just learning—you're growing, evolving, and opening yourself up to new possibilities.

Curiosity is the antidote to fear, perfectionism, and stagnation. When you approach life with curiosity, you're more open to new ideas, less afraid of failure, and more willing to take risks. Just think of it as trying something out. Let's see how that goes. No expectations other than having a new experience.

Stop asking, "Why can't I do this?" and start asking, "What can I learn from this? How can I approach this differently? What's one small step I can take to move forward? What's the worst thing that can happen?"

Brands that stay curious and committed to learning are the ones that thrive. Are you going to be a Blockbuster, or are you going to be a Netflix—or an Amazon?

How to Stay Curious and Keep Learning

Lifelong learning doesn't have to be overwhelming. It's about making small intentional choices every day to stay curious and open to growth.

- **Make Learning a Daily Habit:** Set aside time each day to read, listen to a podcast, or watch a video on a topic that interests you. Even fifteen minutes a day adds up.

- **Surround Yourself with Lifelong Learners:** Join communities or groups where people are passionate about growth and learning. Attend workshops, join masterminds, or start a book club.

- **Embrace a Beginner's Mindset:** Be willing to admit what you don't know and approach new topics with curiosity instead of judgment.

- **Experiment and Explore:** Try something new every quarter whether it's a class, a hobby, or a new way of thinking.

- **Learn from Failure:** Instead of seeing failure as a setback, see it as feedback. Ask yourself, "What did this teach me?"

- **Stay Curious About People:** Everyone you meet has something to teach you. Ask questions, listen to their stories, and learn from their experiences.

Just like these brands (except Blockbuster—RIP, mad respect, and I miss your popcorn tubs), you have to keep asking yourself, "What's next?" Growth isn't about staying comfortable— it's about staying curious.

Change Is Inevitable, Growth Is Optional

Life doesn't always go according to plan. You'll face transitions, unexpected news, and moments where you feel like the rug has been pulled out from under you. Oh, you mean like getting blindsidedly fired during the best year of your career with no severance and a tail between your legs? I'm fine, I'm fine. Everything's fine.

Whether it's a career shift, a personal challenge, or a curveball you didn't see coming, change is inevitable. And, while you can't always control what happens, you can control how you respond.

You can navigate transitions with purpose and grace—no matter how hurtful or painful it was. When I got fired, my first reaction was sadness, then anger, then feeling like I wanted to retaliate and "get justice," and after I sat with the rollercoaster of emotions for a few days, I thought about the identity I wanted to embody. I surrendered it.

And I changed my mindset around what happened. I felt empathy for what the experience may have been like on the other side of the phone call that day. Feeling like my boss HAD to take that action because of some other internal or external pressure I may not have any clue about. And it didn't matter. What's done was done, so I could either burn the bridge to the ground ... or quietly build a new one on stronger ground.

When life throws you a curveball, your first reaction might be frustration or fear, like mine was. But I would encourage you to use some NLP magic and reframe the situation as an opportunity.

- **Acknowledge the Event:** Accept what happened without judgment.
  Example: I got fired.

- **Ask Empowering Questions:** Shift your focus from "Why is this happening to me?" to "What can I learn from this?"
  Example: What role did I play in manifesting this? What message is God/the Universe/Source using this experience to impart on me?

- **Find the Opportunity:** Look for the silver lining or lesson in the situation.
  Example: I've been indecisive about making a career change for a few years, now the decision was made for me, so yay, thanks! Now, I can focus on being intentional about creating a new role or business that aligns with who I'm becoming and who I want to be and what I want to do in this stage of my life and career.

Reframing is about finding a perspective that empowers you to move forward. It's like saying, "OK, this isn't what I planned, but how can I make it work for me?"

You have to be willing to pivot when life throws you a curveball. But remember to stay grounded in your values and let them guide your decisions. It's easy to lose sight of what's important. That's why staying aligned with your mission, vision, and values is so crucial during times of transition. Here's how it helps:

- **Provides a Sense of Direction:** Your values act as a compass, guiding you toward decisions that feel authentic and meaningful.

- **Keeps You Grounded:** When everything around you is changing, your values provide a sense of stability and continuity.

- **Helps You Make Tough Choices:** When you're faced with difficult decisions, your values can help you prioritize what's most important.

- **Fuels Resilience:** Knowing what you stand for gives you the strength to overcome challenges and keep moving forward.

Change can feel overwhelming, but you don't have to do it alone. Break it down, take it one step at a time, and remember—you're stronger than you think. Here are some tools that can help you navigate change:

- **Create a Transition Plan:** Break the change into manageable steps and focus on one thing at a time.
  Example: I'm going to start by updating my resume and networking with people in my industry.

- **Use Anchoring to Stay Grounded:** Recall a time when you felt confident and resourceful. Use a physical anchor to bring

back that feeling when you need it.
Example: Press your thumb and forefinger together.

- **Focus on What You Can Control:** Let go of what's outside your control and focus on the actions you can take.
Example: I can't control whether I get the job, but I can control how I prepare for the interview. I can't control what people say or think about me, but I can control how I think and speak, and what I do next.

- **Seek Support:** Lean on your community, mentors, or a coach for guidance and encouragement.
Example: I know Jane got fired before. I need to talk to someone who's experienced this who I know is thriving now!

- **Practice Self-Care:** Take care of your physical, emotional, and mental well-being.
Example: I'm going to make sure I get enough sleep, exercise regularly, and spend time doing things I enjoy.

Sometimes, all it takes is a shift in perspective to see things in a new light. When you're able to step outside yourself and see the situation from different angles, you can find solutions you never thought possible. Change isn't the end of the story—it's just the beginning of a new chapter. And with the right mindset and tools, you can make that chapter even better than the last.

The Power of Celebration

Celebration is a powerful tool for reinforcing positive behaviors, building confidence, and staying motivated. Take the time to acknowledge your hard work, appreciate your journey, and recognize the person you've become—and are becoming. Here's why it matters:

- **Reinforces Positive Behaviors:** When you celebrate a win, you're more likely to repeat the behaviors that led to that success.

- **Builds Confidence:** Acknowledging your accomplishments helps you recognize your strengths and capabilities.

- **Fuels Motivation:** Celebrating your progress keeps you inspired and energized to pursue your goals.

- **Creates a Sense of Gratitude:** Taking time to appreciate your wins helps you cultivate a sense of gratitude for all you have.

Use your wins to remind yourself of what's possible. When you celebrate, you're saying, "Wow, look at everything I've done! I did this, and I can do it again." Gratitude is one of the most powerful tools for staying inspired. When you take time to reflect on what you've accomplished, you reinforce the belief that you're capable of achieving even more.

How to Celebrate, Be Grateful, and Stay Inspired

- **Create a Celebration Ritual:** Whether it's journaling, treating yourself or your team, or sharing your win with a friend, find a way to honor your progress.

- **Reflect on Lessons Learned:** Take time to think about what worked, what didn't, and what you'll do differently next time.

- **Set New Goals:** Use your momentum to set your sights on the next milestone.

- **Stay Inspired:** Surround yourself with people, books, and experiences that keep you motivated.

- **Practice Gratitude:** Take time each day to appreciate the good things in your life.

- **Visualize Future Wins:** Imagine yourself achieving your next goal. What does it look like? How does it feel? What steps did you take to get there? Who supported you along the way?

Remember, celebration isn't just the end of the journey—it's a crucial part of the process. And with the right mindset and tools, you can make celebration a habit that fuels your growth and inspires you to achieve even greater things. Positive reinforcement is a powerful tool for shaping behavior. When you reward yourself for achieving a goal, you're more likely to repeat that behavior in the future.

Growth is not a one-time event.. It's a way of living, a way of thinking, a way of being. You are a lifelong learner, a resilient navigator of change, and a celebrator of every win. You are a work in progress, and that's a beautiful thing. You're always evolving, always learning, always getting better. The best is yet to come, my friend. I promise.

CALL TO ACTION

IF YOU HAVE *THE REBRAND YOU COMPANION WORKBOOK*, HEAD TO THE SECTION OF THE CORRESPONDING CHAPTER AND COMPLETE THE ASSOCIATED QUESTIONS AND PROMPTS.

Take a moment and think about these three categories and questions.

Learn: What's one thing you've always wanted to learn? How can you start exploring it today? Pick one area of your life where you want to grow. Maybe it's a skill you've been putting off, a topic you've always been curious about, or a hobby you've been meaning to try.

Change: Think about a transition or challenge you're currently facing. How can you reframe it to see the opportunity? What small steps can you take to stay aligned with your mission, vision, and values?

Celebrate: What's one win you're going to celebrate this week? How are you going to reflect on your progress and stay inspired to keep going? Pick one area of your life where you want to celebrate your progress.

I can hardly believe we're already nearing the end of our time together in these pages. But don't worry, this is just the beginning for us! We're definitely not done yet, and I can't wait to see how our connection grows beyond this book. Before you head off to continue your personal Rebrand You campaign, I have a few final thoughts to share in the conclusion. I'm not crying, you're crying ...

Your Rebrand Launch and Evolution

Dabs eyes If you've made it to this point in the book, you're not just *thinking* about a rebrand—you're freaking ready for launch! Maybe you're still scared. Maybe you're still doubting yourself. Maybe you're still waiting for the "perfect" moment, a certain sign, or for someone to give you permission.

Here's your sign. Here's your gentle (but firm) nudge: **Let's get freaking moving on it already, huh?!** *said with an Italian closed-hand gesture*

As you read earlier, I'm obsessed with near-death experience (NDE) videos. Like to the point my YouTube algorithm is probably convinced I'm a ninety-year-old philosopher, or that I am trying to make contact with aliens and angels.

But seriously, I'm fascinated by NDEs.

Why?

Because every single person who comes back from the brink says the same thing: They regret the things they didn't do. The words they didn't say. The life they didn't fully live. Not one of them says, "Wow, I wish I'd spent more time playing it safe and keeping everyone else comfortable."

If you've ever gone down the rabbit hole of near-death experience stories (if you haven't, you should—feel free to DM me for YouTube channel recs), you'll notice the patterns: People describe leaving their bodies, floating above the scene, and being drawn toward a light that radiates pure, unconditional love. Many talk about a "life review"—a kind of cosmic highlight reel where they reexperience not just their own actions, but the impact those actions had on others. And here's what's wild: What haunts them isn't the risks they took, but the ones they didn't. The moments they held back, the times they weren't true to themselves, or when they failed to show love and kindness.

The universal message? It's always about love, authenticity, and living in alignment with your true self. The takeaway is crystal clear: Follow your joy, be real, and don't waste your precious time living someone else's version of your life.

And if that isn't convincing enough for you to get a freaking move on it, allow me to take you back to the car accident I survived. One moment, I'm driving to my mom's house with a fresh mani-pedi ready to head down to Mexico and celebrate love, and the next moment my truck is smashed, and thankfully, I don't have a scratch on me. But the driver who hit me—he wasn't so lucky. A young man in his thirties, with a whole future ahead of him. One moment he was on his way to pick up a bite to eat, and the next moment, he was gone.

No warning. No do-over.

That day, the universe smacked me upside the head and reminded me: None of us is guaranteed tomorrow.

So, what are you waiting for?

We're living in wild, weird, and wonderful times. AI is rewriting the rules of work and creativity. The old "safe" paths are crumbling. Burnout is everywhere, and authenticity is the new currency. The world is screaming for people who are brave enough to show up as their authentic selves, to build lives and careers that truly matter, and to say no to the status quo.

Yes, it's scary. Yes, it's uncertain. Yes, you might fail, or look silly, or have to start over. But you know what's even scarier? Waking up one day and realizing you never even tried.

If the accident, getting fired, and getting sick hadn't happened to me, I probably never would've slowed down to find the truth that I was moving way too fast. Too fast on a path that felt sort of OK, but really wasn't why my soul dropped into this spinning ball of magic in the universe. I kept getting a little closer to my purpose, but not close enough. Until God got impatient and forced me to pay attention to the nudges. Basically, it was like my internal control panel from *Inside Out* was glitching—Joy kept trying to drive, but Sadness and Disgust staged a coup (with Fear riding shotgun) until I finally listened.

I could have continued down the safe path, the trajectory of a corporate executive, but I challenged my limiting beliefs, faced my fears, worked on my mindset, healed my nervous system, took control of my health, and remembered what has been on my heart since I was a teenager. I love marketing, but I have a higher calling and gifts to share beyond the label of "marketing exec." A purpose to serve others through helping, teaching, and inspiring you all to reconnect with your greatest gifts, deepest desires, fullest potential—so you can live the most powerful, abundant life—according to YOUR brand standards.

As AI and technology advance and we learn more about human existence, it's important to stay open to new thoughts, perspectives, and ideas. The beautiful thing is, if you have a clear set of personal brand values, are aligned with who you are, and are tuned into the highest frequency you can each day, you can and will adapt to any platform, any modality, any trend—without losing sight of who you really are. Algorithm be damned! You can change the way you show up in the world, but your core identity—your mission, vision, and values—will always be your anchor.

Your brand is timeless.

Look, the world is moving fast. It's not going to wait for you to get your act together. The only way to keep up—and actually enjoy the journey—is to be intentional about who you are, what you want, and how you show up. It's the key to living a life that feels like *yours*. And I soooo want that for you! I want that for me too!

That's why I created *Rebrand YOU*. The REBRAND Framework wasn't born out of theory—it came from my own life. I created it to help myself get unstuck. To give myself a roadmap when I felt overwhelmed and anxious about where to start. A manual to get my mindset right. A blueprint to guide me toward clarity, confidence, and a sense of purpose.

And now, you have the playbook too. Because I believe many of us are capable of achieving our full potential—sometimes (OK, a lot of times) we just need a clear step-by-step guide to follow. When we're not paralyzed by the "how" or the "when," we can finally take action.

This framework is your starting point. It's your permission slip to treat yourself like the most important brand campaign of your life. Because it is. Because you are.

So, let's recap the REBRAND Framework one more time before we say our farewell-for-nows, my friend:

1. **R**eflect and Research Your Current State: Get honest and informed about where you are and what's working (or not).

2. **E**xamine and Analyze Your Findings: Dig into your patterns, your strengths, your blind spots.

3. **B**rainstorm Potential New Beginnings: Dream bigger. Imagine what's possible.

4. **R**eframe, Reprogram, Rewire: Rewrite the stories and beliefs that have kept you small.

5. **A**ctivate Your Aligned Strategy: Make a plan. Take action. Track your progress.

6. **N**etwork and Build Your Community: Find your people. Ask for help. Reciprocate support.

7. **D**evelop a Growth Mindset: Stay curious. Celebrate your wins. Learn from your setbacks.

No brand becomes iconic overnight. Change happens through small consistent steps. Iconic brands build their reputation over time—one campaign, one product, one service, one customer interaction at a time. The same is true for you. So, don't be too hard on yourself, you damn overachieving go-getter, you! I see you. I am you. We got this.

Here's my final challenge—the mic drop moment: Don't let fear, comfort, or other people's expectations write your story. Rebrand yourself, unapologetically. Be the person who, when your time comes (and it will), can look back and say, "Damn, I lived. I loved. I tried. I grew. I mattered."

You are not too late. You are not too broken. You are not too much or too little of anything. You are exactly where you need to be to begin your next chapter. You now have a step-by-step blueprint to find clarity and take intentional action toward the life you truly want. And remember, you don't have to do it alone. Sometimes, a little extra support can make all the difference in accelerating your journey to a rebranded YOU.

If you're ready for deeper guidance, encouragement, and accountability, I'd be honored to walk alongside you. Explore my coaching, consulting, comedy, keynotes, workshops, and more—whether you're seeking personal transformation or looking to inspire your team or community.

To learn more about how we can work together, flip to the Work with Me section, visit alexiscastorina.com/services, or connect with me on Instagram @alexiscastorina or LinkedIn for ongoing inspiration and opportunities.

You ready? Take the leap. Rebrand *you*. I'll be cheering you on every step of the way.

Resources

We love a good resource around here! This section provides additional tools and materials to support your journey through the REBRAND Framework and your continual evolution beyond this book.

Rebrand YOU—Companion Workbook

You can purchase the companion workbook by visiting **RebrandYouBook.com**. It's also linked in the Resources page of my website at **alexiscastorina.com/resources**.

The *Rebrand YOU Companion Workbook* is designed to complement this book by providing structured exercises and prompts to facilitate the application of the concepts discussed. It serves as an additional resource to help you organize your progress and take actionable steps. The companion workbook is not meant to replace this book. It is intended to serve as an additional resource to help you take action and stay organized. It's also an awesome tool and guide to use with a friend, group, or book club. Why rebrand alone when you can do it with a community and accountability buddies?

Other Resources

For further support and evolving tools, visit **alexiscastorina.com/resources**. This page offers a variety of downloadable worksheets, templates, and curated recommendations to assist you in your personal and professional development.

Work with Me

**Ready to rebrand your life, your team, or your business?
Let's make it happen—together.**

I'm Alexis Castorina—an award-winning corporate marketing executive, speaker, comedian, and entrepreneur. My mission is to make transformation fun for brands, leaders, and careers, and reconnect you to purpose, performance, and profit. With an MBA and certification as a Master Practitioner of Neuro-Linguistic Programming (NLP), Mental Emotional Release®, and Hypnotherapy, my unique frameworks blend neuroscience, marketing communication strategy, humor, and powerful mindset tools to drive lasting change.

Keynotes and Workshops

Energize Your Event, Transform Your Team
My signature talks and workshops are designed to do more than just inspire and entertain—they're designed to deliver growth and lasting change. Whether you want to boost morale, improve communication, or develop leadership skills, I blend humor, storytelling, and proven marketing and mindset tools to help your group regain connection to your mission.

Coaching and Life Design

Clarity, Action, Evolution
If you're feeling stuck or facing a big transition, my coaching is all about helping you reconnect with your authentic self, clarify your vision, and take intentional action toward a career and lifestyle aligned with your values and big dreams.

Marketing and Communication Consulting

Elevate Your Brand, Amplify Your Impact
With two decades of experience in marketing and brand strategy, I help businesses and entrepreneurs strengthen their marketing presence and position. From brand audits to organizational design, I help you elevate your messaging, connect with your audience, and drive real results.

Why Work with Me?

When you work with me, you get more than just ideas—you get energy, clarity, and a partner who's committed to your growth. My approach is practical, creative, and rooted in real-world experience. Whether you're looking to inspire a room, transform your mindset, or take your business or career to the next level, I'll help you unlock new possibilities and move forward with confidence.

What Clients and Audiences Say

"Alexis, WOW! You are a true powerhouse. The way you effortlessly shift the energy in the room and inspire boldness and bravery is incredible. Your unique blend of telling your story and comedy leaves me craving more—I'm hooked!"
—**Event Attendee**

"The biggest value for me was the mindset shift. I started to see myself and my professional experience more cohesively. I gained clarity on my values and what I'm actually looking for in a role and a company. Overall, I feel more confident advocating for myself and asking for what I deserve."
—**Coaching Client**

"Alexis, your message is powerful and will help so many! I will absolutely 10x my laughter because of you! Keep making everyone laugh!"
—**Workshop Participant**

"Alexis is just that person who can see the big picture and execute the details. She helped us build a partnership that was innovative, strategic, and rooted in best practice. She's a true thought leader and an immediate asset to any organization."
—**Marketing Partner**

Ready to Take the Next Step?

Visit **alexiscastorina.com/services** to explore all the ways we can work together, or reach out directly to start a conversation. And if you know someone planning a conference, retreat, workshop, or creative event (or know a friend or colleague who needs career and life design support), your referral means the world to me.

Follow along for ongoing inspiration and opportunities:

Website: **alexiscastorina.com**

Instagram: **@alexiscastorina**

LinkedIn: **linkedin.com/in/alexiscastorina**

YouTube: **youtube.com/alexiscastorina**

Acknowledgments

To my friends and family: thank you for cheering me on through every step of writing and publishing *Rebrand YOU*. When impostor syndrome, perfectionism, and overwhelm crept in (as they do in your girl!), your belief in me and your encouragement fueled me. I'm so blessed to have you in my life. You know who you are. I love you so much!

To Alessia Citro—the best soul sister, mentor, and friend a gal could ask for! Thank you for writing the foreword to this book (and for so much more). The algorithm of the Holy Spirit brought you into my world in the summer of 2024, nudging me to join your book club, share a stage with you at the Speaker Spotlight event, and sign up for your Sedona Soul Scribe Writers' Retreat. You are the definition of an Expander. You truly embody *Higher Self Habits*® (as your first book is so aptly named—and trademarked!). Your story, vulnerability, love of God, and courage to show up fully expressed (the title of your second best-selling book!) have inspired me to lean even further into my own authenticity.

Thank you to all the beautiful souls at the Sedona Soul Scribe Writers' Retreat, hosted by Alessia Citro. Alexus Gouveia, Brie Johnson, Caitlin Hatzenbuhler, Camille Hita, Ginger Mackenzie, Jacque Wilson, Dr. Laura Beltrán-Rubio, Dr. Laura DeCesaris, Erika Peterson, and Laura Kaiser—without you, I'm not sure this book would have ever become more than a dream. Spending five focused days with you in magical Sedona was a gift. I couldn't imagine a better creative container than the collective energy of this special group of women. I'll never forget the experience—or any of you. I can't wait to buy every format of everyone's book that comes out. We are all part of the energy that created these soon-to-be bestsellers, and I can't wait to celebrate you!

A huge thanks to my editor, Laura Kaiser of Word Haven Editorial—the perfect person to work with. You boosted my confidence, validated my idea, and gave props to my writing style, while also challenging me to dial back the parts that were a bit too "extra" (do the kids still say that?) or needed to improve the reader experience. I'm already counting down the days until we work together again on my second book.

Thank you to my book coach, project manager, and fellow writer and creative, Amanda Miller. I'm so glad our "quick" thirty-minute discovery call turned into a ninety-minute conversation where we vulnerably shared stories about our lives, dreams, a little bit of "woo," and, of course, the business of publishing and the authorship process. I couldn't have asked for a better person to help me navigate the unfamiliar waters of publishing a book and all the boxes that need to be checked along the way. Not to mention, you're among the target audience for a book like *Rebrand YOU*—thank you, God/Universe! I'm eager to be among the first to read your book when it's released.

A huge shout-out goes to Laura Duffy, who designed the interior, front, and back covers of my book. Her artistry and strategic eye are truly remarkable, and it's clear why she's worked with the best in the business at Penguin Random House, Simon & Schuster, and HarperCollins. She captured the very spirit of *Rebrand YOU:* a calming, uplifting, blank canvas that evokes peace and creativity, inspiring readers to rediscover who they are and redesign a life that truly fits.

Thank you to my creator and soul family for the continual signs that the path I'm on is aligned for the highest good of myself and humanity. The creation of *Rebrand YOU* is a testament to following your guidance and trusting the clues that help me gain clarity, take action, and evolve into the most loving, compassionate, and authentic version of myself—who's always been there.

Thank you to my comedy teachers, Brian Kohatsu and Tony Vicich. You were both essential parts of my personal rebranding journey, helping me reconnect with my authentic self—the class clown and born entertainer who has always been there, just waiting for a mic. Comedy became a powerful tool for healing from some of the challenges I share in these chapters. Writing jokes about the things I once felt ashamed or insecure about helped me release old energetic blockages and step into a rebranded version of myself—one that proudly includes "comedian" in my expanded identity.

A heartfelt thank you to my attorney, Michael Perry, who was divinely placed in my life during the tumultuous time described in Chapter 1. I'll never forget the calm I felt knowing you had my back when I learned I could be facing a multimillion-dollar lawsuit—just days before Christmas 2022. Your faith and your words, "If you're telling the truth, there's nothing to worry about," brought me so much comfort. Truth is a resonant theme in this book. Being honest with ourselves about what's working and what needs to change is critical, especially in the times we're living in. Thank you for being a protective light during one of the darkest chapters of my life.

And finally, to you—the reader. Thank you for picking up this book and embarking on your own journey of rebranding and transformation. It takes real courage to reflect on your life and intentionally chart a new course. My deepest hope is that these pages serve as a guide and inspiration for you to create a life truly aligned with your highest self. I'd love to hear from you—please reach out and keep me posted on your journey, so I can cheer you on. And if *Rebrand YOU* has positively impacted you, I'd be grateful if you could write a review and share your experience with friends. Encourage them to be as courageous and bold as you were—to reimagine and redesign their lives, with purpose, and on purpose. Just like you did.

With love, gratitude, and laughter, Alexis